Disaster Response

GIS for Public Safety

Gary Amdahl

ESRI PRESS

REDLANDS, CALIFORNIA

ESRI
   Disaster Response: GIS for Public Safety
   ISBN 1-879102-88-9

First printing April 2001. Second printing April 2002.

Printed in the United States of America.

Library of Congress Cataloging-in-Publication Data
Amdahl, Gary, 1956–
      Disaster response : GIS for public safety / Gary Amdahl.
         p. cm.
      ISBN 1-879102-88-9
      1. Disaster relief–Data processing. 2. Emergency management–Data processing. 3. Geographic information systems. I. Title.
   HV553.A47 2001
   363.34'8'0285—dc21   2001001061

Published by ESRI, 380 New York Street, Redlands, California 92373-8100.

Books from ESRI Press are available to resellers worldwide through Independent Publishers Group (IPG). For information on volume discounts, or to place an order, call IPG at 1-800-888-4741 in the United States, or at 312-337-0747 outside the United States.

This book was made possible in part through the generous support of IBM®, a company that has been bringing technology solutions to government for decades, and which has joined with ESRI in many of the case studies presented here to bring a GIS focus to those solutions.

Contents

Other books from ESRI Press

In a world increasingly beset by natural and man-made disasters, it's hard to imagine a more striking or beneficial use of GIS than in matters of public safety. When you stop to consider the number and kinds of disasters that happen at any given moment around the world, the elements and conditions that cause them, the factors and the forces that mix and collide as they occur—and the often indescribable chaos and misery that ensues—the idea of a comprehensive and effective system of response starts to look impossible. But that's precisely what GIS is.

The methods in use right now, at fire stations, emergency management offices, civil defense agencies, and relief organizations, often have their roots not just in precomputerized workplaces, but in the days of horse-drawn fire wagons.

It will come as no surprise to anyone being asked to accomplish more with a slimmer budget that the job (whatever the job may be) has gotten more complicated. This is certainly the case in emergency services and disaster response.

New combinations of forces are not only amplifying the destructiveness of tornadoes, hurricanes, floods, and fires—they are making it more difficult to prepare for and respond to them as well.

One way of thinking of GIS is as a decomplicating machine. With it you can organize, analyze, and display—in all kinds of situations and environments, from a helicopter circling a wildfire to the threshold of a building shaken by a quake and about to be condemned, from the passenger seat in a fire truck to a hundred offices across the country—the increasingly large and complex collections of data, information, and knowledge that make up the reference materials of your average emergency team.

GIS works effectively in all four phases of the disaster management cycle: preparation, mitigation, response, and recovery. Whether analyzing consequences; projecting and predicting; disseminating information; allocating personnel, equipment, and resources; getting from A to B; or picking up the pieces in ways that help rather than hinder stricken families, businesses, and regions, GIS is the tool of choice. It brings people together at just those moments when the forces of nature seek to tear them apart.

Jack Dangermond, president, ESRI

Acknowledgments

My name probably shouldn't be the one on the cover of this book. The names that should be, however, would take up too much space, or have to be set in a font too tiny to see. My work has been easy, and I would like to thank the people who made it so.

Russ Johnson and Brenda Martinez handed me these case studies on a silver platter, and were ready to help every step of the way.

Mike Price and Monica Pratt wrote the original Forest Falls story, which I adapted.

Tim Walsh at Marin County Fire Department, Skip Kirkwood at Tualatin Valley Fire and Rescue, and David Kehrlein at the California Governor's Office of Emergency Services, when asked by me for raw material to fashion stories from,

presented me with hefty and well-written documents. All I had to do was tap them on my desk and square the edges. We can only hope these gentlemen write their memoirs someday.

Tom Patterson of Joshua Tree National Park dropped by my office regularly, rappelling down from one of the helicopters he seems to spend most of his time in to hand me another CD full of information and pictures.

R. W. Greene, my colleague here at ESRI Press, wrote "Extending the Pulaski," and just handed it to me, no strings attached, when I said I needed a story on GeoMAC and its use during the summer of 2000's record-breaking fires.

Cindy Keller at E Team wins the "Fastest Help in the West" award. I'd hit the send button on an e-mail message and

before I could get my fingers back over the keyboard, whatever I'd asked for would be in my mail queue.

Jennifer Galloway produced the book and Michael Hyatt designed it and did the copyediting.

Thanks also to Heather Kennedy and Michael Karman here at the press, for their daily guidance.

Finally, thanks to Christian Harder, *capo di tutti capi,* for giving me a shot.

Gary Amdahl
Redlands, California

The earth may lack volition (at least volition we can comprehend and measure), but it appears to have nearly infinite power over human lives. Mudslides happen, earthquakes, hurricanes, tornadoes, floods, and wildfires happen; one or ten or thousands of people die, and there seems little to do but endure it, fight what can be fought, and pick up the pieces when it's over. Worse, in those places where we might in some small way be able to increase the odds in our favor, we seem to have instead ripped great holes in the ozone, and blanketed the planet with a thick layer of greenhouse gases, raising the mean temperature and altering patterns of weather globally—creating monster storms and setting in motion chain reaction superdisasters.

The president of the International Federation of Red Cross and Red Crescent Societies, Dr. Astrid Heiberg, speaking in 1999, described "a new scale of catastrophe," in which relatively well-understood factors such as global warming and deforestation collide with increasing poverty and growing shantytowns. Red Cross and Red Crescent saw an increase in the number of people seeking assistance in the wake of floods and earthquakes, in the years 1993 to 1999, from less than half a million to more than five-and-a-half million. According to the World Disasters Report 1999, that year was the most disastrous on record.

Conditions in the United States, while markedly different in terms of standards of living, are disturbing as well. Global climatic concerns are the same, but another equally salient consideration is the location of the centers of an increasing population. More and more, these centers of American life are directly in harm's way: homes on unstable, hurricane-prone beaches; nestled in forests regularly burned over by wildfires; in floodplains—or in places like Southern California, a region marked by the confluence of disasters of every description: flood and fire, earthquake and drought. Whatever happens in Southern California and places like it is magnified by the simple fact that there are so many people there, all dependent on a strikingly fragile infrastructure.

Death and casualty tolls and damage costs increased sharply worldwide in the 1990s, particularly as a result of hurricanes, floods, and earthquakes. New conditions like global warming are colliding with increasingly vulnerable populations.

Disaster is, however, susceptible to study, and from that study a good deal is being learned. The level of public awareness and preparedness is rising remarkably worldwide, and new strategies for mitigation, response, and recovery are being developed along a broad spectrum of human activities. Consequent to these changes, funding—from both the private sector and local, state, and federal governments—has increased as well (at least in the United States).

The most remarkable advances, however, have come as computer speeds and capacities make possible new applications and extensions of geographic information systems. The kinds and levels of analysis available now to researchers, policy advisors, and decision makers were only being dreamed of as late as a decade ago.

An average of 845 people died each year between 1900 and 1986 as a result of volcanic activity— far more than in previous centuries—and estimates now put 500 million people at risk. The problem isn't an increase in volcanism, but an increase in the number of people living on the flanks of active volcanoes and in valley areas near those volcanoes.

Claims that computers can make life easier are of course a dime a dozen. The claim that computers can save lives isn't heard quite so often, but still smacks of marketing-speak. It is demonstrably true, however, and it is to that end that this book was put together. Whether planning an attack on a wildfire and coordinating the work of two thousand firefighters, deciding where the best place is to base a paramedic squad, fast-tracking emergency housing grant applications, building grassroots understanding of preparedness in a community, or linking nations from one side of an ocean to the other, the products and services being developed by the people profiled in these case studies make a real difference in the ability of those men and women charged to protect us to do just that.

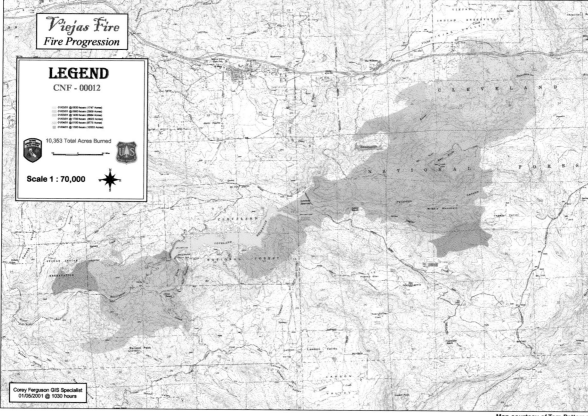

The 2000 fire season was a record-breaker, the worst yet in three decades of steady worsening. Hand-held computers and GPS equipment, used to create this map of the changing perimeter of a fire near San Diego, are making management of big fire-fighting operations considerably easier.

Map courtesy of Tom Patterson

Chapter 1

Forest Falls: A model of a mudslide

RAIN FELL OFF AND ON FOR TWO DAYS on Mt. San Gorgonio. It was early July, monsoon season—or what passes for monsoon in these Southern California mountains. The intense heat of the high Mojave and low Sonoran deserts rises up over the San Bernardino range, finds ocean moisture drifting in from the west, and forms immense thunderheads. Over thirty-six hours on July 9 and 10, about half an inch came down—a lot of rain, to be sure, but really nothing more than fodder for small talk. However, some experienced residents of Forest Falls, a canyon village tucked halfway up Mt. San Gorgonio, found reason to shoot occasional looks of concern peakward, as the streams of muddy water coursing past their homes and down their roads became deeper and faster.

A monster begins to form

On the morning of the third day, July 11, another half-inch of rain came down. The sky lightened for a moment, but another, much bigger storm cell was quickly developing. Witnesses in the valley spoke of a huge black cloud, lit by lightning, that seemed to swallow the mountain whole. The rain came down harder and harder as lightning blasted trees and eardrums. Then, in the space of less than two hours, between two and three inches of rain struck the steep and saturated slopes of Mill Creek Canyon.

Used with permission of the San Gorgonio Wilderness Association and John Cid

High above the smog, noise, and heat of the densely populated San Bernardino Valley: this is the cool, quiet, beautiful countryside in which Forest Falls is nestled—directly in harm's way as well.

Fifty million gallons of water—carrying boulders, pine trees, and mud—came down Snow Creek's drainage alone, into Forest Falls, smashing fifteen homes, suffocating one woman in mud, carrying another off for a mile down the mountain and snapping her bones like twigs, burying a third up to her neck. The torrent picked up house debris, automobiles, and propane tanks and continued down the main road, where it slowed to a halt, leaving a quarter-mile of mud six to eight feet high.

Hundreds of residents, hikers, and daytrippers were stranded in the village, and hundreds more could not return to their homes (and worse, did not know if their homes still existed). Search-and-rescue teams plucked people from the mud and fire crews began to handle the ticking time bombs that the leaking gas tanks had become. Bulldozers were brought up the mountain and began to clear the road, foot by agonizing foot. Sheriff's deputies and highway patrol officers blocked off the only entrance to the village. TV vans and mobile command stations lumbered up California 38, the "Rim of the World" highway. Power was down for only a day, but water was unavailable for five.

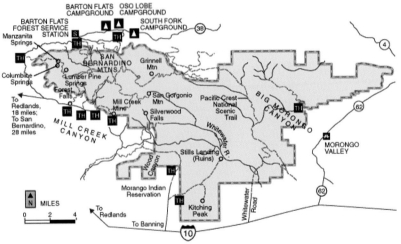

Forest Falls is on the western edge of a wilderness area, putting it at the nexus of conflicting needs for unspoiled beauty and public safety.

How could such a thing happen?

The sequence of events in Forest Falls during the two hours of rain and the few minutes of the slide is now much more clearly understood, thanks to modeling by Mike Price, mining solutions manager for ESRI in Redlands, who happened to be hiking on San Gorgonio the day of the disaster.

The first question Price posed was broad: What combination of elements could account for the intensity of the storm and the extensiveness of the damage it caused? Was it an anomaly, a freak disaster? Or was there an identifiable chain of cause and effect?

Forest Falls is strung along the sides of Mill Creek Canyon, a feature created by seismic activity: a finger of the San Andreas Fault, the Mission Creek strand, is at work here, rapidly sliding one block of the San Bernardino Mountains upward against another. It's not hard to imagine the village having a big bull's-eye painted at its center—the steep and steadily eroding sides of the canyon have a history of coming unglued—but while there have been numerous flows and pile-ups of debris, the scale of the July 1999 disaster was unprecedented.

Mt. San Gorgonio modeled with ArcView® 3D Analyst™. The fatal mudslide happened in Mill Creek Canyon, on the lower right side of the image. The location of Forest Falls is indicated by the box.

Looking for data in all the right places

Looking for data on which to base his modeling, Price found that nearly everything he needed was readily available—much of it free, and the rest inexpensive. What he couldn't find, he created from existing data using ArcView Spatial Analyst. A Forest Service hiking map and a U.S. Geological Survey 7.5-minute quadrangle map of the Forest Falls area were scanned, registered in the universal transverse Mercator (UTM) projection in the North American Datum for 1927 (NAD27), and entered into the database.

These maps provided "you are here" and landmark points of reference. To build the models, digital elevation model (DEM) data was needed. Price went to the USGS EROS (Earth Resources Observation Systems) Web site: there it was, free for the asking. Using the Raster to Grid utility in ArcView GIS 3.2, he converted the USGS data and added it to the model in the form of a grid. Elevations were then classified and ramped by color.

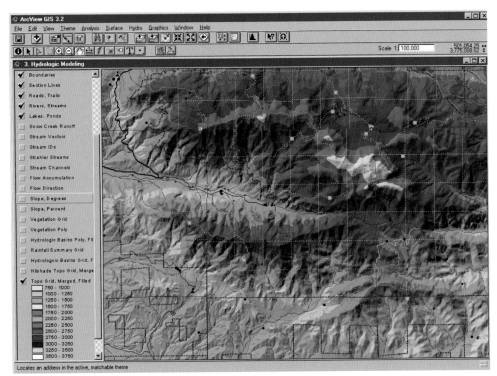

This is the Mill Creek Canyon area viewed according to a hillshade theme, converted from free USGS data in ArcView Spatial Analyst.

Slope, hillshade, and the angle of repose

Slope and hillshade were the next factors to be considered. Slope is a matter of degree and stability of surface; hillshade is a matter of perspective, combining azimuth and altitude—that is, the sun's height in the sky and compass point on the horizon. The quality and quantity of sunlight an area receives obviously affects the kind of vegetation that will grow there, and the extent of that growth. Steepness of slope is a factor as well, and also plays an important role in determining if and where structures should be built. If there are no unusual circumstances, slopes of 15 degrees or less are considered reasonably safe for building.

The angle of repose, beyond which resting, stable material will begin to move, is about 35 degrees. Price's models showed large areas of unstable terrain in and around Forest Falls. Some slopes were nearly vertical, tilted at 80-degree angles.

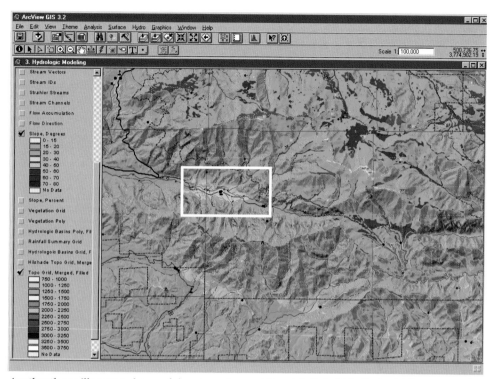

Another theme illustrates degree of slope in and around Forest Falls (within the box). The orange color indicates slopes of 30 degrees or more, and the blue, between 20 and 30. There is virtually no flat or even gently sloping land in Forest Falls.

A clearer picture emerges

To more precisely understand the lay of the land, and the course the flood took over it, Flood Insurance Rate Map (FIRM) data, obtained from the Federal Emergency Management Agency (FEMA), was scanned and registered. This data made it possible to show one-hundred-year floodplain areas, flood zone designations, roads, and drainages.

More data from the EROS site was downloaded and added to the model as well: roads, section lines, and wilderness boundaries were now part of the model.

Using DEM data and the Hydrologic Modeling Sample extension of ArcView GIS, watershed patterns and stream networks were added to the picture to establish direction of flow and location of sinks. Sinks are places on the mountain (individual cells or spatially connected cells in the elevation data) where flow cannot be determined—usually because of easily correctable errors in the data. Once these sinks were filled in (a matter in most cases of simply choosing the Hydro > Fill Sinks option), the paths that excessive flow would take in the area became clear.

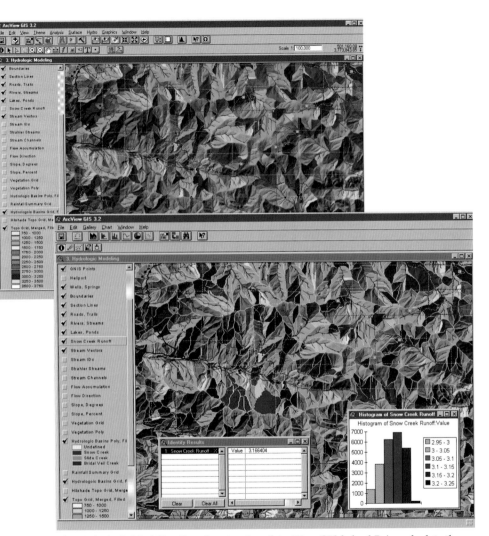

The Hydrologic Modeling Sample extension of ArcView GIS helped Price calculate the directions in which water would flow. The properties of these watersheds can then be assimilated in a single attribute table, which can in turn be easily used in a number of other applications.

The crucial element

Data from the California GAP (Geographic Approach to Planning) Analysis Project, which classifies land according to the type of vegetation that dominates an area (Sierra and Mixed Conifer, for instance, or Mixed Chaparral), proved to be the conclusive factor in the inquiry.

The San Bernardino Mountains have extraordinarily diverse species of flora—among the widest ranges of any Southern California mountains. Joshua tree, pinyon pine, and juniper can be found at lower elevations on eastern slopes, with chaparral on the western. Coulter, Ponderosa, and Jeffrey pine, white fir, incense cedar, sugar pine, black oak, California dogwood, and bigleaf maple take over as you ascend. Nearer the tree line are stands of lodgepole pines, and here and there, on dry, rocky, windswept crags, limber pines.

Much of Forest Falls is densely forested, but a large area near the Snow and Slide Creek drainages has almost no vegetation at all—nothing, in other words, to absorb the force of a flood, in exactly the places where it was needed most.

According to Doppler data supplied by Kavouras: a DTN Company (which deals in meteorological data worldwide), the Snow, Slide, and Bridal Veil drainages received as much as an inch more of rain than the rest of the Forest Falls area: three inches to the two that fell in immediately adjacent areas.

ArcView Spatial Analyst can reproject Doppler radar data as a grid. These images show clearly that while the whole area received a lot of rain, the three principal drainages into Forest Falls got even more—up to three inches.

A hundred million gallons

Price was able to estimate the amount of water moving through the three drainages by making them separate polygons and running the rainfall theme over them. The fifty million gallons that came down Snow Creek were responsible for most of the damage to homes, the injuries, and the death. Half that amount came down Slide Creek, but the 40-degree slope and lack of ground cover caused a flow of logs, boulders, and mud to surge down the village's main road, a pileup of debris six to eight feet high and a thousand feet long. Thirty-five million gallons came down Bridal Veil, too, but the relatively dense vegetation on that slope mitigated the destructiveness of the flow.

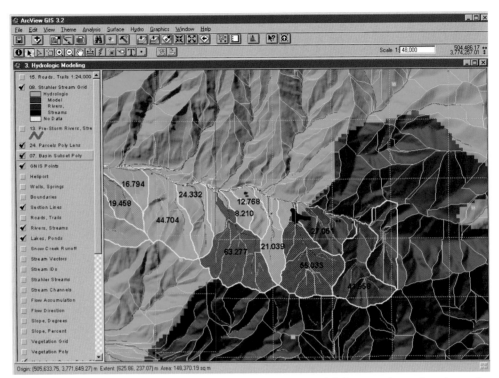

Separate polygons for the three drainages were compared with rainfall data to estimate the volume of water moving through the village.

Modeling before and after a disaster

Measures designed to prevent the disasters that can be prevented, to temper the ones that cannot, to respond to and recover from either kind—all these depend increasingly on transmitting information that changes as quickly as the circumstances, and on integrating that information. GIS models of what happened in a disaster, physical histories, and levels of descriptive data from bedrock to treetop can be turned around to predict what will happen the next time volatile forces of nature combine in disaster, helping people to get out of the way and stay out of the way.

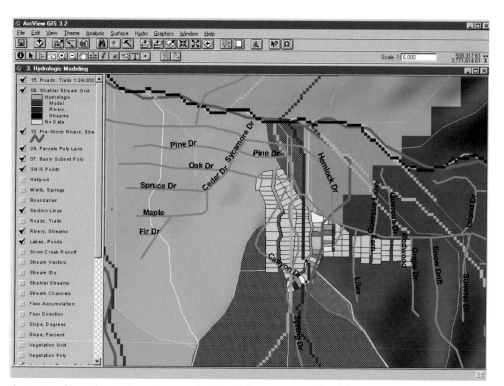

A street and parcel map shows how much of the slide area was residential.

Acknowledgments

Thanks to Mike Price, mining solutions
engineer, ESRI.
E-mail: mprice@esri.com

Thanks to Monica Pratt, editor, *ArcUser*™.
E-mail: mpratt@esri.com

Chapter 2

Tualatin Valley Fire and Rescue

MANAGERS OF MUNICIPAL FIRE DEPARTMENTS and emergency medical services are dealing with a mandate—to do more with less—that may not be unique to their business, but which is certainly magnified by the nature of it: saving lives and protecting property.

Tax-reduction initiatives, burgeoning needs for new kinds of local government services, and demands that whatever is being done be done better and faster, are complicating the lives of fire and EMS chiefs across the country. As they decide where stations ought to be sited, what kind of equipment to deploy in a given situation, and how to allocate other resources, educated guesses have had to do.

GIS is beginning to change that norm. Response times are dropping, costs are being reduced, and, perhaps most important of all, as budgets are negotiated, managers can make vivid, compelling, and persuasive arguments as they present their cases—for a little more than the lot less they've got to work with—to the councils and committees controlling the purse strings.

In Beaverton, Oregon, a suburb of Portland that includes both farmland and urban development, Tualatin Valley Fire and Rescue (TVFR) has put GIS to use in several innovative ways that illustrate the directions in which the technology can be taken.

Tualatin Valley Fire and Rescue found itself at a crossroad: limited resources and funding, and an increasingly complicated district to protect.

The changing face of data

The nature of the fire hazards to which a municipality is susceptible determines strategies for suppression. Resources, in other words, are deployed where it seems they will do the most good. Conditions, however, do not necessarily stay the same from year to year. As communities grow, it becomes particularly important to maintain fire hazard data at a level of accuracy that allows decision makers to consider needs and circumstances as they are, not as they have been.

Building size and type is the primary consideration. Performance standards mandated by organizations external to the fire service, such as the Insurance Services Organization (ISO), a risk analysis group, and the National Fire Protection Association's standards group, influence strategic decisions as well. Using GIS, TVFR can map its area of responsibility according to these various criteria. Tall buildings, buildings with particular fire flow patterns, buildings housing hazardous materials, and other features of real property can be pulled together in a single picture, allowing the service to quickly group and isolate hazards, analyze current deployment strategies, and develop new ones.

Fighting a suburban house fire calls for tactics and equipment that would be less effective if the fire were in a tall building storing hazardous materials. TVFR's district of ten diverse communities presents challenges for resource allocation.

Ladder trucks, amoebas, and cookie cutters

ISO requirements, for instance, call for a ladder truck to be located within two-and-a-half miles of all buildings two or more stories in height. The organization awards a full credit rating if this requirement is met. Proportional credit is granted based on the percentage of tall buildings covered within a given area. Clearly, the ideal scenario has all the tall buildings in a community within the two-and-a-half-mile response area of one or another of the ladder trucks. The TVFR fire district, however, spans ten communities; given a budget with sufficient funding for only a limited number of such trucks, the question of placement becomes critical.

Two hours and three steps of GIS work later, the problem was solved.

The first step was to geocode the locations of all buildings two or more stories tall. Once these locations were on the electronic map, ArcView Network Analyst was used to create amoeba-like overlays showing the patterns of response of all stations in the district. The final step was to move these amoebas around the map like cookie cutters, trying to include as many tall buildings as possible in each space. By moving ladder trucks to three different stations, the district's coverage of tall buildings was improved nearly 100 percent.

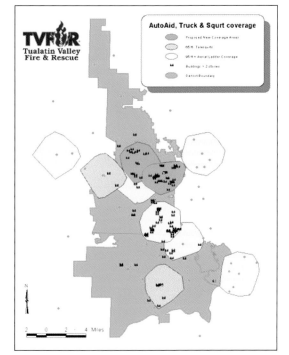

Matching ladder trucks to the locations of buildings two or more stories tall, TVFR was able to maximize credit from the ISO.

Location, location, location

In the days of horse-drawn fire wagons, a map and a compass were all a chief needed to plan station sites: the one-and-a-half- to two-mile radius was the standard area of responsibility. In many cases it remains the standard today. Newer elements that have been included in the planning mix are often too narrow in scope, or oversimplified in their assumptions: fire departments protect only real property, travel speed is constant at all hours of the day, emergency events occur randomly with respect to time, and so on.

GIS analysis suggests that most of these assumptions are simply not so. For instance, a significant part of a fire department's workload may not relate directly to the fighting of fires, involving instead medical or non-emergency responses. Travel times pretty clearly change over the course of a day, and, surprisingly, emergencies occur more predictably than common sense might have us believe.

These variables make the testing of potential station locations difficult. Driving around in a fire truck with a stopwatch and marking times on a paper map may not even keep a station within the ballpark as communities grow and change almost overnight.

As suburbs expand and change, new stations have to be built and old ones re-sited to ensure complete, effective, and fair coverage of the district.

The station on a dead-end street

As Portland and its suburbs grew, TVFR found itself serving several cities out of stations that had been built in older, pre-annexation fire districts. Some of these sites did not fit the reorganized district as well as they needed to. One station, in fact, after a major highway construction project was completed, had become the only fire station in the United States on a two-way dead-end street.

Again using ArcView GIS and Network Analyst, the department was able to simulate drive times over the entire district at different times of the day and with varying traffic conditions. With drive-time parameters more clearly established, areas of coverage for proposed station sites stood out more sharply, too. Once GIS analysis was complete, TVFR built a new station in a place that at first glance might not have seemed appropriate: farmland—but farmland that has very quickly become an area of high-density multifamily housing.

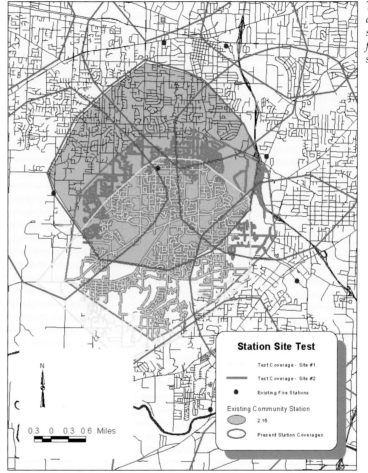

This map shows drive times and station coverages for two potential station sites.

Station Site Test

Test Coverage - Site #1

Test Coverage - Site #2

• Existing Fire Stations

Existing Community Station

2.15

Present Station Coverages

N

0.3 0 0.3 0.6 Miles

Jaws of Life

One of the most useful ways GIS can be used in fire and rescue operations is to geocode individual incidents and display them on map backgrounds, or with pins on actual wall maps. Patterns and hot spots quickly emerge, allowing fire and EMS staff—as well as other interested parties, such as injury prevention advocates—to allocate resources where they will do the most good.

TVFR decided several years ago to keep its Jaws of Life equipment near entrances to several freeways, where, it was reasoned, higher speeds resulted in greater damage to vehicles. The GIS-generated pin map showed this not to be the case: there were more serious incidents—ones that required extrication—at the intersections of major surface arterial roads.

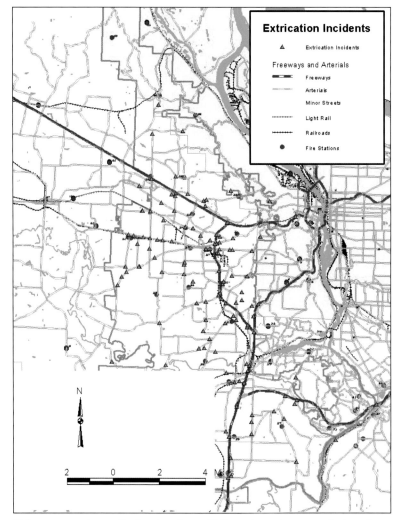

This map geocodes accidents where Jaws of Life equipment was required, and shows a higher rate of incidence in places where it was not expected.

Peaks and valleys

"Pure fire" organizations are disappearing. In their place are fire departments providing emergency medical services, hazardous material expertise, and technical rescue capability. Staffing strategy has changed, too. The traditional method called for static and uniform deployment of firefighters in twenty-four-hour shifts. The conditions underlying this strategy were building construction and lighting practices that made fire a round-the-clock problem, and much shorter distances between homes and workplaces.

The new deployment model is the Peak Activity Unit (PAU), which is based on the locations and activities of people, rather than on types and locations of buildings.

TVFR uses its GIS in a continual process of examining PAUs and adjusting work schedules. For instance, part of the TVFR district is the commercial center, where concentrations of workers and activities are very high during the standard working day, and very low otherwise, when expanding commutes take workers farther and farther away from city centers. Using ArcView Spatial Analyst to geocode and perform density analyses on an hour-by-hour basis, TVFR is able to schedule human resources with the same effective precision it uses in allocating equipment and siting stations.

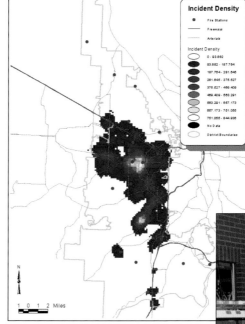

Using Peak Activity Units, a model of people and their activities over time, rather than of building type and location, TVFR was able to adjust its work schedule to match more closely the times and places where fires were starting.

Acknowledgments

Thanks to Skip Kirkwood at Tualatin
Valley Fire and Rescue.

E-mail: kirkwoha@tvfr.com
Web: www.tvfr.com

Chapter 3

Marin County: Mapping risk

THERE ARE MORE THAN ONE HUNDRED THOUSAND HOUSES in Marin County, California, situated in towns, villages, ranches, and farms, across some of the most beautiful country our continent has to offer: six hundred square miles of coastal cliffs and tidal flats, meadows, hills and mountains cut through with deep canyons, and cool, quiet forests of redwood and pine. The Golden Gate is at one end, and the Pacific Northwest at the other.

The only catch is that the beautiful landscape is also a "high-fuel zone"—a particularly dangerous place to be when wildfires ignite. Increasingly high concentrations of people and structures in what is essentially wilderness—the urban–wildland interface—make the possibility of disaster even greater.

The Marin County Fire Department (MCFD) has countered this growing threat by using GIS to analyze prevailing conditions, assess risks, and model wildfire scenarios that not only help firefighters to fight fires, but communities to plan expansions and maintain properties in ways that prevent and mitigate the destructiveness of uncontrolled blazes.

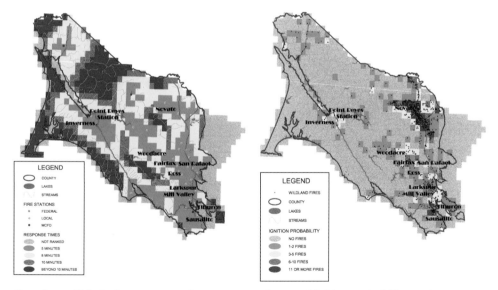

Two views of Marin County you won't see on postcards: a graphic history of wildfires and response times.

The California Fire Plan

GIS first began to be used by fire and related agencies as a way of sharing and managing information about natural resources. The trend culminated in the mid-1990s, when many federal, state, and local wildfire agencies began conducting protection assessments. The California Department of Forestry and Fire Protection published the California Fire Plan (CFP).

The CFP was a foundation on which funding and staffing for a revamp of wildland fire assessment throughout the state could be built. The idea was to train firefighters with experience in the field to use GIS. Drawing on both resources—the old know-how and the new technical can-do—they would be better able to assess the areas for which their departments were responsible, and determine where trouble spots were located. Once these areas had been identified as definite and demonstrable wildland fire threats, various preventive measures could be designed and put into action: prescribed burns, shaded fuel breaks, and neighborhood fuel reduction drives, for example.

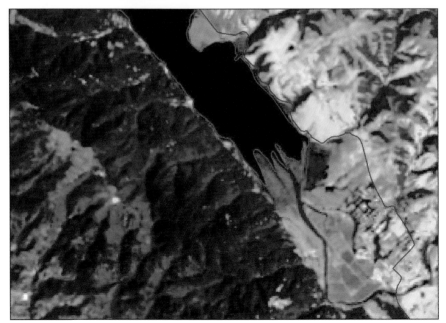

Aerial and infrared photography of Marin County provides base images over which more specific and detailed maps can be laid.

The final four

Four factors determine the severity of a wildland fire and its consequences in a given area: the amount and types of hazardous fuel or vegetation, past levels of service, weather patterns, and the number and kind of assets or values at risk.

Fuels

A hazardous fuel is anything that's highly combustible. Generally speaking, in wildland fires, combustibility depends on the kind of vegetation that dominates an area. The MCFD determined highly specific areas of dominance by referring to several sources of information. Studies were used from Humboldt State University, the United States Forest Service, the California Department of Forestry and Fire Protection, the California Department of Fish and Game, and the Marin Municipal Water District. These studies were queried and compared to infrared imagery. Each study was entered into the department's database and became a GIS layer with a specific emphasis. For example: the CDF study included detailed information about hardwood trees, the Fish and Game data concentrated on riparian areas, and the water district had the best coverage of redwoods within its watersheds.

The United States Forest Service (top), California Department of Fish and Game (center), California Department of Forestry and Fire Protection (bottom), and other organizations provided data on land cover, each with a different emphasis.

Validating vegetation

Once this data was collected and stored in readily accessible GIS layers, it had to be verified and validated by field observation, or changed to reflect actual conditions. A laptop computer, the Tracking Analyst extension of ArcView GIS, and a means of getting around the countryside were all that were needed. As a road or path was driven, a track was simultaneously drawn on the screen through an area designated specifically as, say, redwoods. What firefighters could see was compared to what was represented on the map. ArcView Tracking Analyst allowed changes to be made quickly and on the spot. With vegetation maps modified and validated, they could be converted to fuel model maps, where the theme or emphasis is no longer the type of tree or land cover, but that tree or land cover's combustibility: how likely would a fire in this area be to spread, how quickly and intensely would it burn, and to what extent?

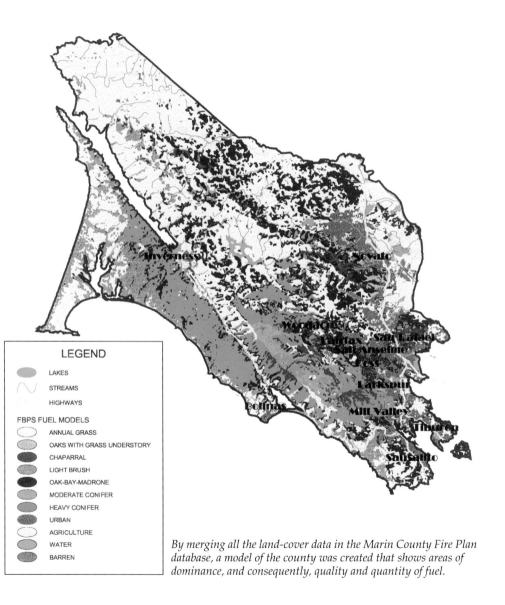

LEGEND

- ⬭ LAKES
- ∿ STREAMS
-   HIGHWAYS

FBPS FUEL MODELS
- ⬭ ANNUAL GRASS
- ⬭ OAKS WITH GRASS UNDERSTORY
- ⬭ CHAPARRAL
- ⬭ LIGHT BRUSH
- ⬭ OAK-BAY-MADRONE
- ⬭ MODERATE CONIFER
- ⬭ HEAVY CONIFER
- ⬭ URBAN
- ⬭ AGRICULTURE
- ⬭ WATER
- ⬭ BARREN

By merging all the land-cover data in the Marin County Fire Plan database, a model of the county was created that shows areas of dominance, and consequently, quality and quantity of fuel.

The steeper the slope, the faster the fire

The extent and intensity of a wildfire depends on the topography of the land it's burning up. Fire moves across flat land more slowly than fire on a mountainside. With the vegetation maps converted to fuel models, the next step is to create a slope map. Ten-meter digital elevation models (DEMs) are downloaded from the U.S. Geological Survey Bay Area Regional Database (BARD). Using ArcView Spatial Analyst, these DEMs are converted into slope models with six values used for ranking. A slope between zero and 10 percent receives a rank of 0. A slope between 11 and 20 percent receives a rank of 1, and so on.

The final step in building the fuels map is to combine the slope rank and the fuel model. A fuel rank is given to each 450-acre cell in the area. Although cells this big might seem unwieldy or possibly misleading, the size conforms to all the fire plans in the state, and has proved effective in practice.

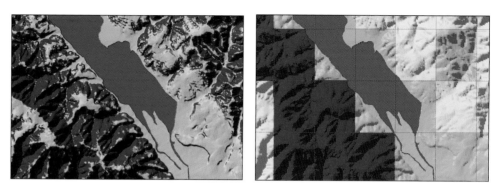

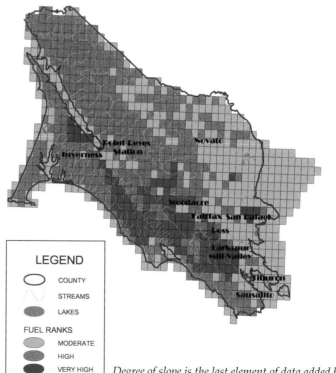

LEGEND

◯ COUNTY

〵 STREAMS

⬤ LAKES

FUEL RANKS

⬤ MODERATE

⬤ HIGH

⬤ VERY HIGH

Degree of slope is the last element of data added before the county is divided into 450-acre cells. The result is a fuel-ranking map.

Level of service

Level of service, the second phase of a
risk assessment program, is an analysis of
the way fires in specific places have been
fought in the past, and the consequences
of each. The goal is to identify areas
where fires would be most costly in terms
of suppression (it's not hard to spend a
million dollars a day) and damage to
property. Information is gathered from
comprehensive response reports filed
by every fire agency in the county.
Addresses are geocoded to spatially
locate each response. Once the responses
are on the map, dates and times of occur-
rence, vegetation types, acreage consumed, and causes are compared, and,
using ArcView Spatial Analyst, density
maps are created indicating those areas
where (and periods of time when) calls
for help are highest. Other conditions and
constraints can then be laid over the
basemap: potential losses, travel times
to the fire, historical occurrences, and
resistance to control.

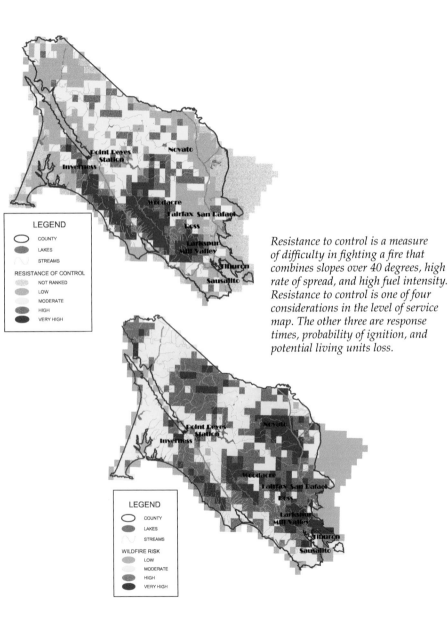

*Resistance to control is a measure
of difficulty in fighting a fire that
combines slopes over 40 degrees, high
rate of spread, and high fuel intensity.
Resistance to control is one of four
considerations in the level of service
map. The other three are response
times, probability of ignition, and
potential living units loss.*

Fire weather

The role weather plays in wildfires is dramatic and unpredictable. Marin is particularly susceptible to variations in the weather: the influence of marine air, solar radiation on some slopes, and inversion layers have their own special effects on basic weather patterns. Strong north or northeast winds put the entire county at risk, but these winds sometimes happen several times in a season, and sometimes not at all.

The MCFD developed a fire weather ranking system in which inversion, aspect, sheltering, and the location of weather-monitoring stations are the variables.

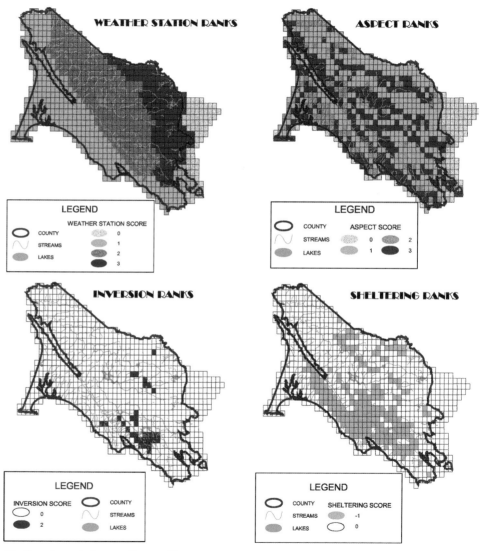

The four elements in a weather-ranking map.

The inversion layer is simply a warm body of air that traps cool, moist, foggy air below it. Above it—its altitude is about eleven hundred feet—warm, dry air encourages fires to burn. Below it, fires are less likely to spread.

Aspect is the direction a slope faces. South-facing slopes tend to be dryer, with highly combustible brush and grass. North-facing slopes are more moist, and supportive of conifer forests, which burn more slowly.

Sheltering refers to the beneficial functions of tree canopies. If the canopy is sufficiently dense, it will collect moisture and allow it to be leached into the soil. The most dense canopies can even block sunlight and prevent high-fuel vegetation from growing. Wind speed and direction are also affected by the quality of the canopy.

The last factor in weather ranking is the location of the six weather stations in Marin County, which record and combine air temperature, relative humidity, and wind speed in a single value.

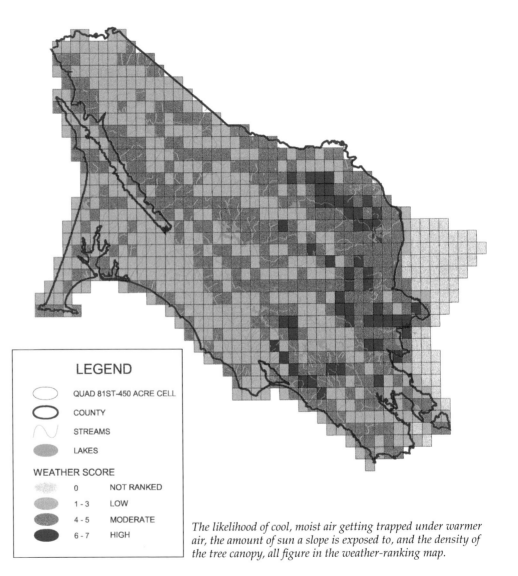

LEGEND

⬭ QUAD 81ST-450 ACRE CELL

◯ COUNTY

〰 STREAMS

⬭ LAKES

WEATHER SCORE

⬭ 0 NOT RANKED

⬭ 1 - 3 LOW

⬭ 4 - 5 MODERATE

⬭ 6 - 7 HIGH

The likelihood of cool, moist air getting trapped under warmer air, the amount of sun a slope is exposed to, and the density of the tree canopy, all figure in the weather-ranking map.

Assets at risk

Once the fuel model, level of service analysis, and weather ranking are in place, the quantity and quality of the assets and values at risk need to be determined. In the Marin Fire Plan, an asset is defined as anything that someone wants protected from wildfire. Because the average price of a home in Marin is $600,000, the potential dollar total for coverage of losses is quite high.

In addition to structures (such as homes), MCFD identified six other categories of assets and values:

1 Wildlife (the Mount Vision fire of 1995, for instance, almost wiped out the beaver population in Point Reyes National Seashore)

2 Soil-stabilizing vegetation that reduces the potential for flooding

3 Water supply (75 percent of Marin's drinking water comes from county watersheds)

4 Soil (erosion can become more severe after a fire)

5 Recreational areas (thirty-eight businesses dependent on tourist dollars lost significant business because of the Mount Vision blaze)

6 Rangeland (ranching is the largest form of agriculture in the county)

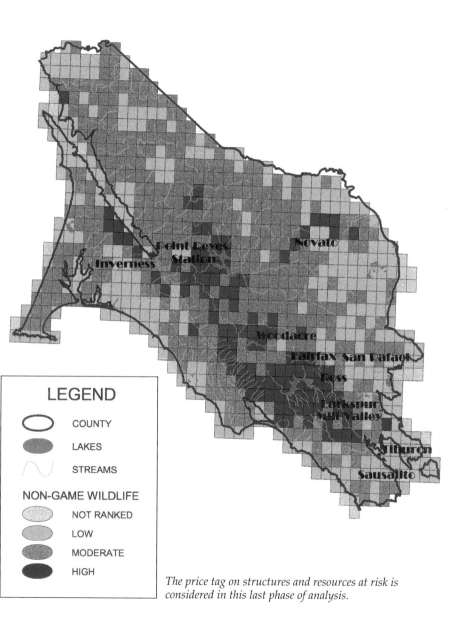

LEGEND

⬭ COUNTY

⬬ LAKES

∿ STREAMS

NON-GAME WILDLIFE

⬬ NOT RANKED

⬬ LOW

⬬ MODERATE

⬬ HIGH

The price tag on structures and resources at risk is considered in this last phase of analysis.

After the modeling is over

The action plan that has emerged in the wake of MCFD's intensive mapping and modeling work has a number of fronts: ignition management, fire engineering, land-use strategies, public education, and vegetation management.

Ignition management is a process of comparing fire cause to fire prevention measures. By creating a fire cause density map, prevention measures can be targeted to a specific cause. For example, if an area has a high density of fires caused by children playing with matches, a good question to ask is where is the nearest school and when is the last time a fire prevention and education program was performed. If there is a high percentage of equipment-caused fires, maybe "spark arresters are required" signs need to be posted on the main travel routes.

Temporal trends can also be determined. If, over a given period of time, wildland fires happen repeatedly in the same area, there may be a hidden—or at least not obvious—cause. Are the fire stations too far apart? Due to urban development, have more ignition sources moved into an area? Have repeated fires in a particular area changed the dominant vegetation to the point where fires will become more and more severe? All of these questions can be analyzed using GIS.

Fire engineering is a concept that deals with ways defensive and preventive control measures can be built in: strategically placed fuel breaks, properly maintained fire roads, defensible space around dwellings, fire-safe roofing materials, and land-use planning (that is, codes that restrict the kinds of structures that can be built in areas where risk is great). When these ideas are implemented according to GIS-generated analysis, they are remarkably and demonstrably effective means of fighting fires.

Acknowledgments

Thanks to Fire Captain Specialist Tim Walsh at Marin County Fire Department.

E-mail: twalsh@marin.org

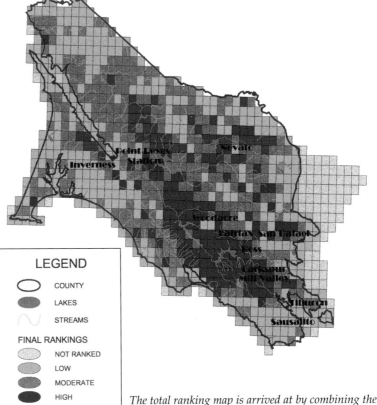

LEGEND

⬭ COUNTY
⬭ LAKES
∿ STREAMS

FINAL RANKINGS

⬭ NOT RANKED
⬭ LOW
⬭ MODERATE
⬭ HIGH

The total ranking map is arrived at by combining the asset, fuel, weather, and level of service rankings.

Chapter 4

E Team: Emergencies and the Internet

ONE OF THE GREAT THEMES of the Age of Information is that of making information usable. Waves of raw data crashing in on someone trying to make an important decision in the middle of a hurricane can almost seem like a cyber-replication of the disaster, not a way of coping with it. In a world where jobs are increasingly interdependent, whether public- or private-sector, the sharing of data and the management of knowledge have become the hallmarks of solving complex problems like disasters.

Not surprisingly, one of the most important trends in disaster management revolves around new ways to share information. Instead of ten agencies operating in a vacuum and telling each other what they're doing only when and if they can find the time, you have ten agencies doing what they do best and automatically, instantly keeping each other apprised of situations and actions as they develop—a well-oiled machine.

The Internet is the ideal medium for such exchanges, but "putting it on the Web" is easier said than done. Static reference material is one thing—data changing from minute to minute is another. Designed originally to facilitate communication during the greatest catastrophe imaginable, a nuclear strike, E Team has found a way to make the Internet the backbone for sharing information in all kinds of emergencies.

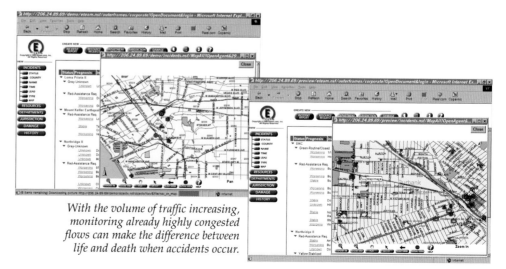

With the volume of traffic increasing, monitoring already highly congested flows can make the difference between life and death when accidents occur.

Island hopping

Matt Walton, president and CEO of E Team, says that historically, emergencies and disasters have in effect put managers on islands. "Everybody did his or her job in isolation. There was no easy way for everyone to be involved and be effective."

In September of 1999, after nearly a decade of research and development, E Team released E Team Government Edition, a software system that facilitates the accurate, efficient, and safe sharing of data—particularly when conditions are not at all conducive to calm deliberation and comprehensive planning.

All E Team software products rely on ESRI's ArcIMS® for visual display of current events and changing situations. The user calls up a map with color-coded and symbolized icons representing types and severity of incidents, then clicks on an icon to get specific information concerning status, background, resources already assigned and employed, the lead agency, and other important facts about the event.

Police and fire departments, EMS providers, and local and state emergency operations centers can enter and participate in a common digital information environment that functions in real time, using whatever hardware and databases they already have in place. Interface is also possible with federal agencies, such as the FBI, the National Guard, and FEMA. Finally, public agencies and private companies—who actually supply 80 percent of the resources called for in response and recovery efforts—can draw from the same detailed fund of knowledge, and communicate with each other directly, continuously, and clearly.

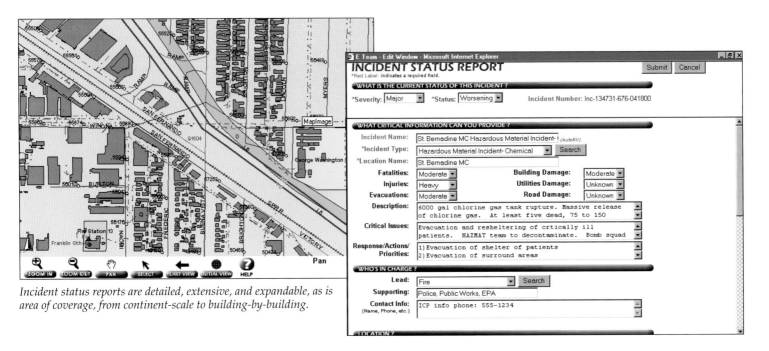

Incident status reports are detailed, extensive, and expandable, as is area of coverage, from continent-scale to building-by-building.

ASP ASAP

Users of E Team's disaster management products can buy and install the software themselves, or can opt to have E Team act as an application service provider (ASP). In the latter case, users access E Team software over the Web, with no need to install software or configure servers; all that's required is a PC and a standard Web browser such as Netscape Navigator® or Microsoft® Internet Explorer.

The application environment is scalable and can expand to meet both the requirements of organizational growth and the extraordinary demands of any particular emergency. It can also be easily customized to suit existing structures, with departmental, group, and position names, equipment and facility picklists, and so on. Replication, authentication, and encryption are handled by Lotus® Domino, as well as other Internet and proprietary security tools.

The facility is hardened and tough to crack, the security architecture is multi-layered and the data fully protected, the servers are load balanced, monitoring is in real time, and there is no downtime.

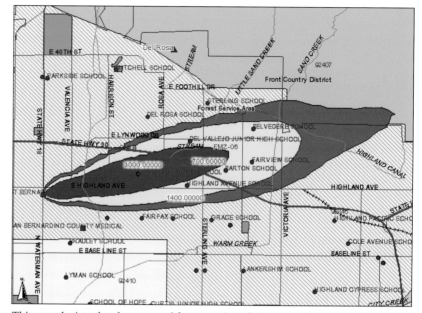

This map depicts the plume spread from a toxic spill. To access this information, all a user needs is a PC and a Web browser.

From sea to shining sea

The U.S. Department of Transportation—which oversees, among other things, the greatest engineering feat in the history of the world, the U.S. interstate highway system—adopted a customized version of E Team software to help it deal with the Y2K rollover.

USDOT's Office of Emergency Transportation needed a way of monitoring the status of the entire country's transportation systems, and contracted with several consultants in the course of a search for the means of acquiring real-time or near-real-time information on such a vast scale.

The most useful product the office employed was the E Team Activation Information Management (AIM) system. AIM's reporting differed in three crucial ways from USDOT's routine methods of data collection. It could handle input from thousands of modal entities at once; it could provide information not only on problems and disruptions, but report where no problems were occurring—that is, where the infrastructure was intact and working smoothly (important news in the midst of alarmed overreaction, hysteria, and false rumors); and finally, it worked as a central clearinghouse, allowing USDOT analysts to pass information along to department policy makers and other federal coordinating agencies.

"Effective management of transportation resources in emergencies is a core mission of the U.S. Department of Transportation," says Bill Medigovich, USDOT's director of emergency transportation. "AIM, based on E Team's suite of software, enhances our disaster management capabilities by enabling our emergency personnel to interface with regional, state, and local emergency personnel to share critical data in real time through the Internet. This significantly reduces our disaster response time, mitigating the physical and economic consequences of transportation emergencies."

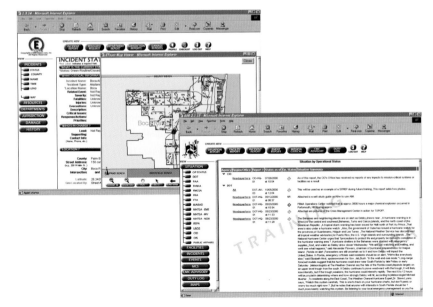

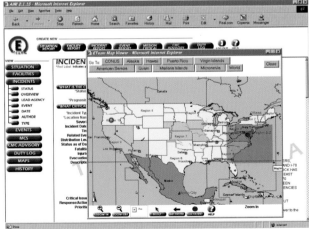

The U.S. Department of Transportation used E Team software to monitor the Y2K rollover, using real-time status updates and general and specific maps to keep tabs on virtually the whole country's transportation network.

Highways of the future and to the future

Because AIM has monitoring capabilities that are so broadly applicable, and because it uses the Internet as a principal medium, USDOT believes its utility will only continue to expand, helping the department deal with large-scale natural disasters, major protest events (such as the December 1999 World Trade Organization demonstrations in Seattle), acts of terrorism, and even cyberterrorism.

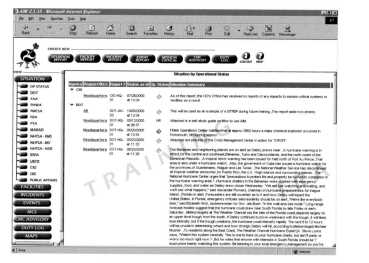

USDOT sees opportunities for broad applicability of E Team software, running the spectrum of potential disruptions of flow.

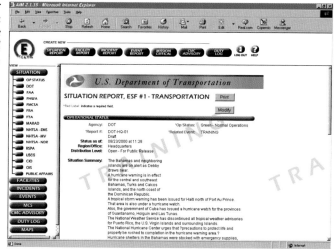

Acknowledgments

Special thanks to Cindy Keller.

Web: www.eteam.com

Chapter 5

Winston–Salem: Integrated Network Fire Operations

SOMEBODY SMELLS SMOKE and yells *"Fire!"* The alarm in the station goes off. Firefighters may not slide down the pole into their boots anymore, but they still have to jump into the truck and drive to the fire. They still have to hit the sirens and the lights and fight traffic. And they still have to come up with a plan of attack in a matter of minutes.

Finding out where the fire is and getting there has never been easy, and quick response times have always been critical to success. But as cities grow, finding fast, straightforward routes has become a complicated job; and with concomitant development of technologies and industries involving increasing use of hazardous materials, the nature of fire itself is changing.

Current practice is based on radio dispatch and hard-copy reference manuals. While the driver blasts the rig in and out of congested intersections and hauls it around tight corners, the firefighter in the passenger seat handles the radio and one or two big three-ring binders stuffed with information—the assimilation of which can sometimes mean the difference between life and death.

Radio dispatch and hard-copy reference materials have in the past been the only means of getting firefighters briefed and to the scene quickly. In Winston–Salem, North Carolina, they have trucks equipped with touch-screen computer terminals.

Vital information at the tip of your finger

In Winston–Salem, North Carolina, the ride is still full of g-forces, jolts, and bangs, but in place of the three-ring binder with pages falling out is a touch-screen laptop. In addition to a street centerline file generated with GPS equipment and used as a basic routing framework, GIS software loaded into the laptop displays the address of the alarm; the best route at the moment (taking into account temporal factors such as jams, accidents, and roadwork); the locations of hydrants, schools, streams, and railroads; simple icon links to building diagrams, floor plans, and prefire survey and hazardous materials information; multiple-address locations (apartment complexes, for instance); and special needs—such as those of the residents of a nursing home.

The project is called Integrated Network Fire Operations (INFO), and the Winston–Salem Fire Department won an international award for its pioneering effort.

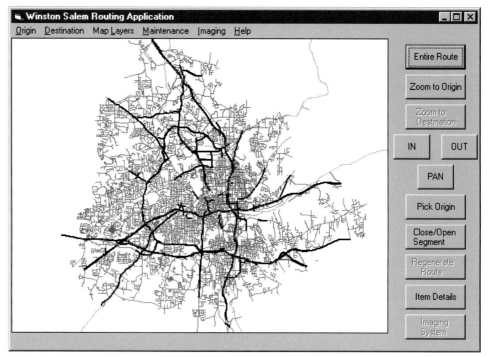

The basemap for the Winston–Salem Fire Department's Integrated Network Fire Operations, on which successive layers of information can be laid.

Mobile network terminals with sirens and flashing lights

The Winston–Salem Fire Department covers a territory of 106 square miles and serves a population of more than 170,000. There are 254 firefighters and twelve people working in support, spread out over seventeen continuously occupied stations.

Electrocom MDT System Proposed Configuration Mobile Computer

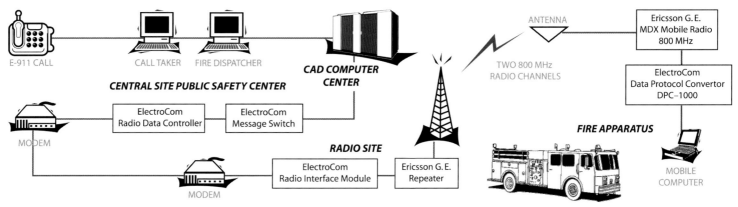

Winston–Salem's Integrated Network Fire Operations (INFO) connects every phone in the city to every fire truck in the department.

These seventeen stations are connected to the City of Winston–Salem's Fiber Distribution Data Interface (FDDI) network via ISDN circuits. Each station has a PC and a T1 Internet link. Twenty-eight fire trucks are in turn connected via shock-proof, laptop mobile data terminals.

Fire Station ISDN Network

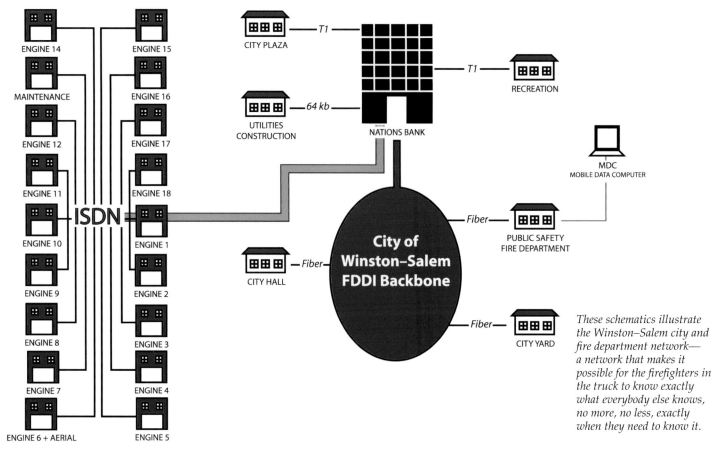

These schematics illustrate the Winston–Salem city and fire department network— a network that makes it possible for the firefighters in the truck to know exactly what everybody else knows, no more, no less, exactly when they need to know it.

Getting from A to B and B to C

Let's return to the ringing alarm. Captain and driver jump to their truck, where they consult the onboard monitor. The location of the burning building and a potential route are already on display. As soon as they know whether to turn left or right out of the station, they are underway.

The captain now evaluates the route the computer has suggested. It looks like a good one, so they follow it. But at a major intersection, they find power lines down and the road blocked. By simply tapping the right buttons on the monitor screen, they can close off the rest of the route, reset the origin to match their current location, and generate a new route.

Written directions and route mileage can be displayed, and the map of the entire route can be zoomed in on and out of as questions or problems arise along the way.

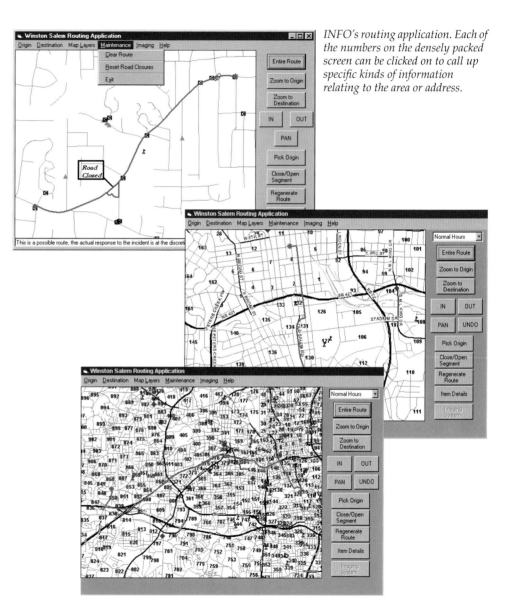

INFO's routing application. Each of the numbers on the densely packed screen can be clicked on to call up specific kinds of information relating to the area or address.

Need to know

Once questions about route have been answered, the captain can focus on the specifics of the fire to which they are heading. Again, all that's required is a fingertip to the screen on the Imaging System bar: HAZMAT, physically challenged, multiple-address, and all available prefire survey information is instantly displayed.

Acknowledgments

Thanks to Julia Conley and Tim Lesser, Information Services Department, City of Winston–Salem.

Web: www.ci.winston-salem.nc.us/fire

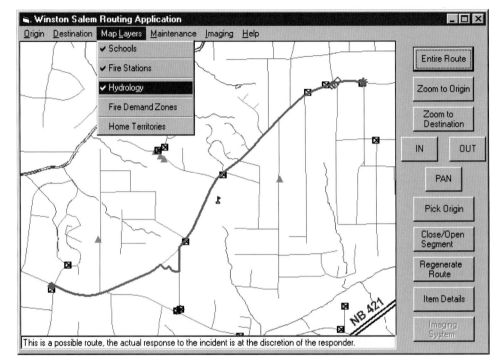

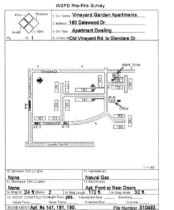

These screen shots show rivers, creeks, fire hydrants, schools, and prefire surveys. The themes, or kinds and quantities of information stored in a system like the W–SFD's INFO, are virtually unlimited.

Chapter 6

National Fire Protection Association: Firewise Communities

THE NORTH AMERICAN ECOSYSTEM uses wildfires to regulate and renew itself. Fire archaeologists have estimated that before European settlement commenced, between 4 and 11 percent of the continent burned annually. The frequency could vary widely from subsystem to subsystem—fire return in the Everglades, for instance, was estimated at five to ten years, while nearby in the mangrove system it was five hundred to a thousand years—but 4 percent of North America is seventy-five million acres.

Compare that figure with the nearly seven million acres consumed in the disastrous summer of 2000. Then compare that to the nearly two million of 1973.

The story of wildfire on this continent in the twentieth century is an interesting and important one. Told and heard by enough people in the right places, it will affect not only the future of our natural environment but our national—even hemispheric—economy as well.

After a century-long decline, occurrences of wildfires have made a sharp turn upward.

Photos courtesy of Tom Patterson

A brief history of fire

R. Neil Sampson, a senior fellow with
the Forest Policy Center, writing in the
National Fire Protection Association's
newsletter, *Wildfire News and Notes,* likens
the story to a sharp U-turn. Around 1900,
wildfires were relatively large and relatively common: logging practices, arson,
and nearly nonexistent attempts at suppression all played parts in the phenome-
non. So did a smaller population—
particularly in the heavily forested mountain West—and the patterns of that population's growth. Then, beginning in the
1920s, and picking up speed after World
War II, consciousness-raising campaigns
on the part of the American Forestry
Association and advances in suppression
techniques and technology rapidly
decreased the average number of acres
burning every year.

From 1900 to the early 1970s, the numbers went steadily down. Then came the
U-turn: increasing numbers of bigger and
bigger fires, a sharp rise in the number of
homes in the wildland–urban interface,
conflicting interests, political scrutiny,
finger-pointing, and skyrocketing suppression and damage costs. The summer
of 2000 looks to have been something like
a billion-dollar affair.

Photos courtesy of Tom Patterson

*Firefighters are better
than ever at suppressing
wildfires, but more and
more homes are in areas
of high risk.*

A necessary evil?

Wildfire is clearly a good thing and a bad thing at the same time, necessary but disastrous. We cannot—and should not—eliminate it from the natural cycle of life, but try saying that to someone whose home has been destroyed—to a hundred people whose homes have been destroyed, or to the family of a firefighter who died in the line of duty.

A compromise with nature needs to be reached, and it's to that end that the NFPA and other associated members of the National Wildland/Urban Interface Fire Program have developed a workshop called "Firewise Communities."

Between a rock and a hard place: The ecological need for the renewal of wildfire and the destructive consequences of same reached a climax in 2000 with the Los Alamos fires and the later Montana blazes.

Firewisdom begins at home

The plan is straightforward and geared toward small groups and individuals, who will acquire some basic knowledge about the nature and behavior of fire, and some skills in dealing with it at the community level—then take that knowledge back into their communities and help educate their neighbors.

The underlying idea is that grassroots networks are the most effective way of transforming risky neighborhoods and areas into safer bets. The benefits are numerous, various, and mutual: preserving the quality of life; driving down the costs of prevention, suppression, and recovery; building a customer base or improving a corporate image—all this under the umbrella of saving lives and protecting property.

The National Fire Protection Association's Firewise Communities program is a way of bringing concerned citizens face to face with the realities of wildfires before they happen.

A new approach to fire problem identification

The tools of the workshop are interactive and reflect the new technological resources available to educators, planners, and policy makers: CDs, videotapes, and GIS. As the issues central to public safety and community planning become more complex—and often more sensitive, politically and culturally, too—the use of hard-copy maps has had to give way to the big databases and swift access to information that computers provide. Not only are hard-copy maps limited to static depiction of conditions, but production costs make widespread use—the cornerstone of Firewise Communities—prohibitive as well.

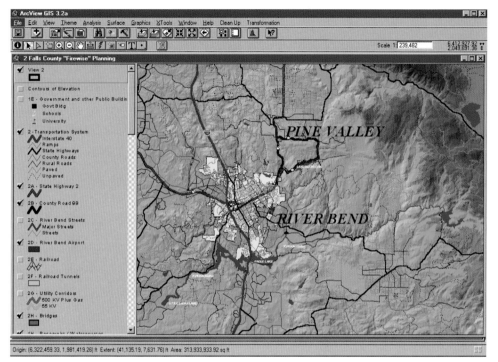

Vast amounts of easily stored, transported, and shared information make GIS an indispensable tool in the study of wildfire.

The all-purpose view

Land use and land cover are the basic determinants of fire behavior. To understand which areas of a community are at risk, to what degree, and why, it's necessary to view the landscape from several different perspectives.

First you need a general map of the here and now, what planners call a Base Year Map: streets; roads; railways; utility corridors; ground area covered by buildings; agricultural land; commercial and noncommercial forested areas; and undeveloped land are all represented.

Upon this foundation you build successive layers of information—that is, the same piece or pieces of land viewed from different perspectives created by querying the GIS software for views based on other data sets.

By researching resources such as city and county public works departments, state planning offices, county assessors, highway and fire departments, utility districts, and federal agencies like the USGS and U.S. Census Bureau, it's possible to create an extraordinarily detailed, nearly complete virtual community that can be viewed and analyzed on a palmtop computer.

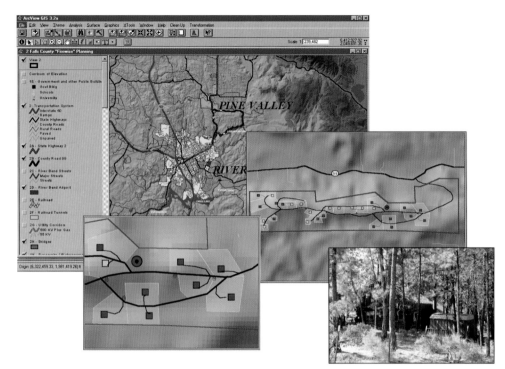

GIS makes analysis possible on several levels at once, from county overview to subdivision, street level to individual structures, as well as according to a large variety of themes.

Biology, demography, ecology, economy, geography, geology

Land can be viewed according to the fuel content of the vegetation that dominates a particular area. Tall, thick trees, for instance, spaced widely apart in acidic or rocky soils, constitute a zone of low fuel content. Dense stands of short trees in heavy brush make for a high-fuel zone.

The lay of the land must be considered as well. Fire travels fastest uphill, and slowest across flatland. Homes that can be reached only by crossing a ravine on a makeshift bridge, or by making a steep climb, are at considerably more risk than homes more traditionally situated.

Density of dwellings, their ages, and types of material used in their construction comprise another possible view. Buildings can also be classified according to function: commercial, industrial, institutional, residential—with these classes subdivided into more detailed descriptions: residential structures can be identified as single-family dwellings, mobile homes, duplexes, apartment buildings, and so on. Hotels, restaurants, malls, factories, hospitals, schools—all these varieties of structure can be displayed with specific icons linked to tables of data.

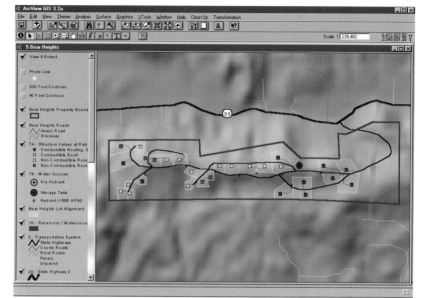

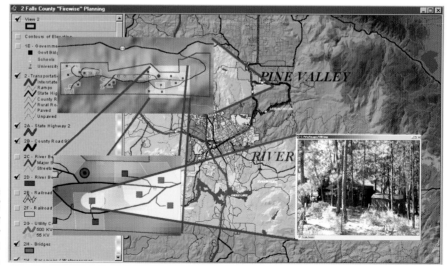

These two ArcView GIS screen captures demonstrate how information can be "called out." The first deals with combustible roofing materials and the location of water supplies, while the second homes in on a single dwelling—complete with photograph.

Projects, views, themes

The possibilities for quality and quantity of information become almost infinite at this stage of GIS organization: the only limits are the processor speed, disk space, and memory of your computer, and the availability of base data. The number of jobs a particular business provides, assessed values of property, unemployment rates, mean income—even data on salaries for fire department personnel, education levels, insurance premiums, costs associated with past fires, predictions for the consequences of fires in the future—all this information and more can be included in your database.

The exercises performed by Firewise Communities workshop participants are based on three ways ArcView GIS stores, organizes, and displays data: the project, the view, and the theme.

The project stores and organizes all the information needed for the task at hand, as well as resulting output (maps, charts, and tables). Projects use components called documents to organize and display information in different ways. One type of document, the view, displays sets of geographic data called themes as interactive maps.

In the workshop, data about a fictional "Falls County" is stored and organized in a project. Workshop participants can select various views of the county— towns, cities, neighborhoods, wilderness areas, and so on—for closer study. Each view in turn contains a number of themes—fuel models, slope models, land use, communication and transportation infrastructure, water sources, flood zones, fire station locations, and more—that participants can display interactively.

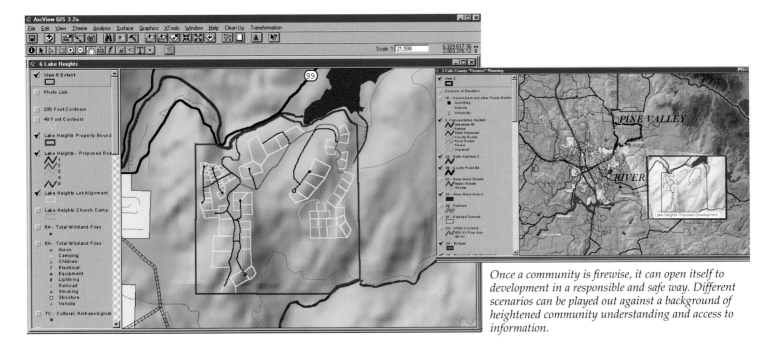

Once a community is firewise, it can open itself to development in a responsible and safe way. Different scenarios can be played out against a background of heightened community understanding and access to information.

NFPA 299 Standard

The goal of the exercise is to fill out a Wildfire Hazard Severity Form Checklist as completely as possible. Using GIS in conjunction with the "NFPA 299 Standard for the Protection of Life and Property from Wildfire," and an appendix to same, "Wildfire Hazard Severity Analysis," the general nature and level of risk for the homes and businesses of a community can be assessed. The task then becomes one of finding locally acceptable ways to reduce risk, and building up a comprehensive proposal to be shared with municipal decision makers and the community at large. Minimum acceptable standards can be prepared that address structural hazards (location,

material, design), fuel hazards (defensible spaces within high-fuel zones), miscellaneous hazards (structure density, slope, and other kinds of dangerous topography like chimneys and canyons, weather patterns, and fire history), and additional considerations like road widths, grades, and surfaces, bridge widths and weight limitations, water supplies, and utility locations.

An immense amount of data comes under scrutiny in a Firewise Communities workshop, which is why the use of a GIS is integral to the process. A GIS is inherently graphic in nature—it's a sorting, analyzing, and illustrating machine, in other words.

The issues that need to be understood, the plans drawn up, the cases persuasively made are just as inherently visual in nature. "Seeing clearly" is another way of "understanding." Wildfires appear to be, and to some extent are, unpredictable, uncontrollable forces of nature. But the truth is they operate according to physical laws. They are necessary occurrences whose outcomes are increasingly predictable. As more and more people study their communities, as more and more data enters the public domain and is used effectively, the less and less likely it is that homes, businesses, and lives will be lost when the inevitable happens.

In the end, Firewise Communities programs are another way of bringing together people with common needs, and opening the door to a network of geographic information that affects their daily lives in concrete ways.

Acknowledgments

Thanks to Jim Smalley, manager,
National Wildland/Urban Interface
Fire Program.

Web: www.nfpa.org

Chapter 7

2015: A Montgomery County, Maryland, odyssey

MONTGOMERY COUNTY IN MARYLAND, named after one of Washington's generals, is one of the nation's oldest (chartered in 1776), most affluent, densely populated, and swiftly growing counties. At just under a million, the population has almost doubled since 1970, with a huge jump happening between 1980 and 1990. It is second, in total population, only to Fairfax County in Virginia, of all jurisdictions in the Washington, D.C., metropolitan area. This growth has put more than ordinary pressure on the county's fire and rescue service to maintain a high level of responsiveness.

The dawn of GIS

In one of its first attempts to use GIS to assist the county's fire and rescue service, the Montgomery County Department of Information Systems and Telecommunications (DIST) took a basic road map, pinpointed a station, and overlaid it with fire alarm box areas and station response areas. In this way a verifiable sense of the practical limits of vehicles housed at each station in the county began to grow.

Thirty-three miles from Baltimore and fourteen from the heart of the District of Columbia, Montgomery County, Maryland, is situated in one of the eastern seaboard's main power corridors. This early example of a GIS map (at the right) shows roads, fire stations and their response areas, and fire alarm box areas.

The big leap forward

A major qualitative change in the way the usefulness of maps was perceived happened with the switch to data orientation. Using ArcView GIS, a complete history of fires fought from 1991 to 1995 was mapped. Incidents were aggregated by each of the thirty-three stations' response areas, and color coded. Hot, warm, and cool spots were immediately recognizable.

The first rescue squad relocation study

The first major systematic analysis of geographic information undertaken by the Montgomery County Fire and Rescue Squad (MCFRS) was the Rescue Squad Relocation Study. The GIS team, using ARC/INFO® on a Sun® UNIX® system, examined the time it was taking for existing squads to get to wherever they were needed. Calculations were made with aggregated population figures and circles with radii of five miles. The goal was to determine how much of the population was actually covered, where stations overlapped areas of response, and, most importantly, where the gaps were.

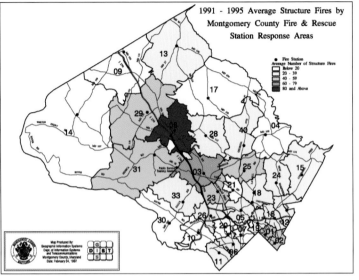

This more sophisticated GIS map ranks station response areas by the average number of fires within their borders over a five-year period.

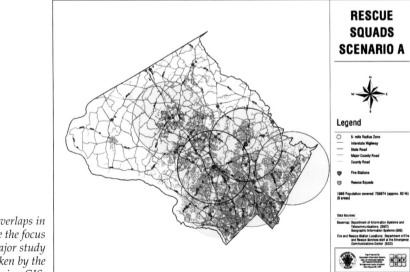

Gaps and overlaps in coverage were the focus of the first major study undertaken by the MCFRS using GIS.

Fire trucks don't fly

Examining the five-mile travel map, the GIS team realized it was looking at a major misstep: fire and emergency vehicles do not go as the crow flies, but on roads like everybody else. Using ARC/INFO and the ArcView Network Analyst extension, the team discovered that coverage wasn't nearly as good as it had first thought: the number of people receiving adequate service dropped by as much as 20 percent when actual road routes were created in place of the five-mile circles.

Back up to speed

Learning from its mistakes, the GIS team found response to the Rescue Squad Relocation Study quite encouraging. In the wake of its success with county planners and politicians, another study was commissioned. The Fire–Rescue Response Study explored response times for the thirteen stations in the county equipped with advanced life support (ALS, as distinguished from BLS, Basic Life Support) units.

Assuming two-and-a-half minutes would be necessary for 911 call processing, dispatch announcement, and turnout of a crew, six-minute limits for each medic unit were mapped.

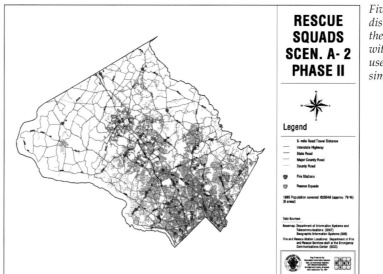

Five-mile travel distances are again the focus here, but with actual roads used, rather than simple circles.

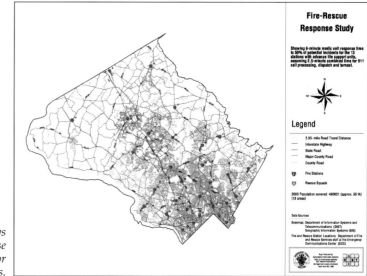

This map shows six-minute response time coverages for thirteen stations.

Water

Montgomery County is urban, suburban, and rural in character. Its southern and eastern reaches, bordering on the District of Columbia, have municipal water, but some rural and suburban areas are dependent on wells. The MCFRS uses tanker trucks to supply firefighters in these areas. Location of these trucks can obviously make a big difference when water is scarce: thus the Water Supply Study.

Bestseller

One of the most popular and regularly requested GIS maps shows aggregations of fire and rescue incidents. Each fire box area in the county is classified according to the number of incidents that take place there each year, and is color ramped.

The optimal locations of water tankers were arrived at with the help of this map, a product of MCFRS's Water Supply Study.

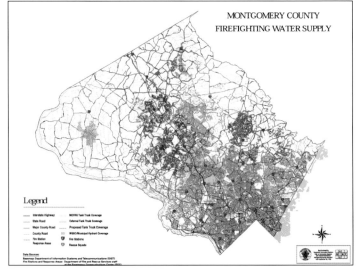

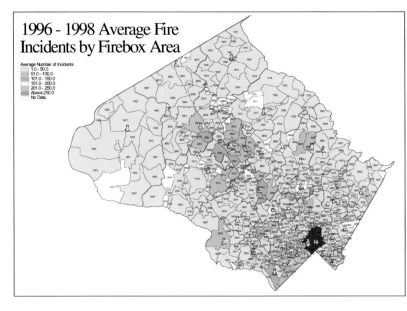

Fire and rescue incidents aggregated by fire alarm box area.

Water Supply Workgroup

As population grows, so grows traffic. The more traffic, the greater the likelihood of accidents. The faster the flow of traffic, the greater the chance of multivehicle smashups and serious damage: highways, particularly interstates in heavily populated corridors such as the one in which Montgomery County is situated, become the scenes of incidents requiring fire and rescue crews. And of course water supply is not the first thing planners think of when considering problems and solutions on highways.

Unlike surrounding jurisdictions, Montgomery County does not have hydrants on its limited-access routes. The county's Water Supply Workgroup proposed construction of dry standpipes at each over- and underpass. It then requested maps showing sections between each bridge divided into thousand-foot subsections—a thousand feet being the maximum distance a single pump engine can pump water— thus indicating the places where additional engines would be necessary.

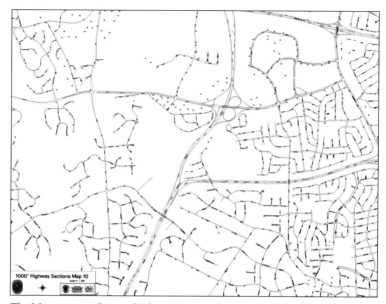

The Montgomery County highway system, showing distances from over- and underpasses in thousand-foot sections.

A major study and a big surprise

On the heels of successes with the Water Supply Study, the Fire–Rescue Response Study, and the Rescue Squad Relocation Study, a commission came for a major new project, the Station Location/ Resource Allocation Study. The goal was to decide where a new station in the rapidly growing Clarksburg–Germantown area should be located.

Using ArcView GIS and Network Analyst on a Dell® PC running Microsoft Windows NT®, numerous maps were created for each station in the area, showing increasing travel distances and times to each neighborhood in Clarksburg–Germantown.

With existing stations mapped, new sites were proposed, projected, and analyzed. Conclusion? If guidelines established by the MCFRS for the minimum acceptable coverage were adhered to, not one but three new stations would be necessary.

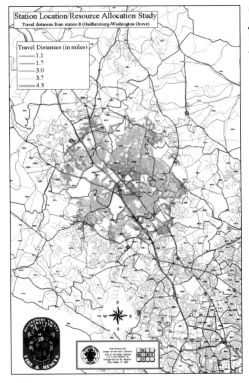

Generated as part of a study of a rapidly growing area of Montgomery County, this map led decision makers to a startling conclusion.

And the winner is . . .

A fundamental reference in the county's master plan for an anticipated addition of more than two thousand residential land parcels, the final map in the Station Location/Resource Allocation Study initiated a new phase in county planning. Station locations in the past had been based on availability of public land, and according to precedent, the rules of thumb that had guided decisions in the past. There was, consequently, little attention paid to fastest responses possible to the greatest number of people.

The goal illustrated in this map was to get emergency vehicles and personnel to 90 percent of the population within five minutes—figuring three miles at thirty-five miles an hour—and 50 percent of the population within seven minutes—four and three-tenths miles at thirty-five miles an hour.

Along the way, the GIS team won an award at Towson University's GIS Conference map competition, as the "Most Communicative Map of 1999."

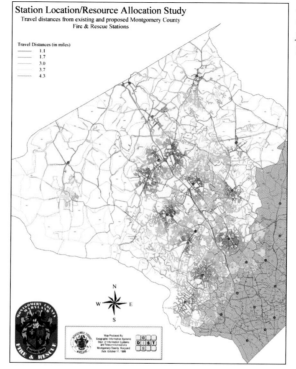

Station Location/Resource Allocation Study
Travel distances from existing and proposed Montgomery County Fire & Rescue Stations

Travel Distances (in miles)
1.1
1.7
3.0
3.7
4.3

An award-winning map showing travel distances from both existing and proposed stations.

2015

Having handled the present pretty adroitly, the GIS team turned its attention to the future. Parts of Montgomery County were growing (Clarksburg–Germantown–Potomac, for instance, in the northwest, farther from D.C.), and parts were drying up (Silver Spring, on the D.C. border in the southeast). Maps taking into account both current densities and projections of density in 2015 were called for.

Acknowledgments

Thanks to Tim Taormino, Geographic Information Systems, Department of Information Systems and Telecommunications, Montgomery County, Maryland.

Web: gis.co.mo.md.us/gis/about.htm

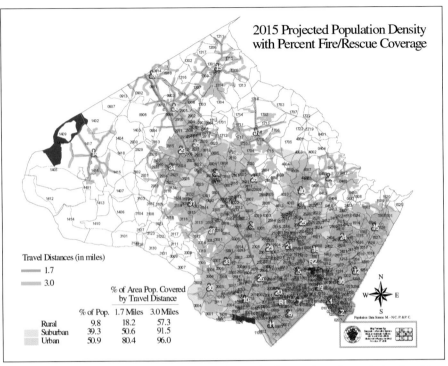

This map takes into account not only present urban, suburban, and rural population densities, but predictions of growth and decline for the next fifteen years.

Chapter 8

Extending the Pulaski

THE CERRO GRANDE BURN in the spring may have been an omen that the fire season of 2000 was not going to be normal. Cerro Grande began peacefully enough as a controlled burn, but quickly overwhelmed its handlers to become New Mexico's worst fire disaster ever. Much worse was to come. By late summer, there was conflagration across the western United States and by late autumn when it was all over, almost seven million acres had burned, more than twice the annual average—destruction on a phenomenal scale. A disaster of such magnitude compelled fire managers to look everywhere for help, to think in new ways. From this need came a nation-sized wildfire GIS system that provided interactive maps on the World Wide Web to fire managers in any location—letting them, and the public, see not just where every fire was burning in the country, but also its size and its potential for destruction. With GIS, they could make strategic decisions about deploying fire-fighting resources in a way they had never been able to before.

Technology's march sometimes seems inexorable, but there are some areas where computers and software have yet to make much of a dent. Fighting forest fires, for example, doesn't require a big bag of subtle technological tricks. To be sure, there are lots of vehicles and lots of aircraft, though many are of a decidedly low-tech, DC-7 vintage. But on the ground, the tools used for fighting a fire are about as fundamental as fire itself. One of the most basic is the Pulaski, a short-handled combination axe and hoe, used for cutting through brush and earth to create fire lines. It's a stout, brutal tool, exactly what's needed to battle a wildfire of similar brutality.

Fighting fire with paper

But low-tech has its limitations. Maps, for instance, are essential for assessing the geography around a wildfire, and for tactical planning. Most firefighters still use paper ones effectively.

They also use tape and scissors—to cut and paste these government-issue topographic paper maps together to make one that fits the actual area in which they're working. In 2000, some fires were so big they encompassed 120 such maps.

Fire raging all around them, elk take refuge in a fork of Montana's Bitterroot River, in August 2000.

John McColgan/Alaska Fire Service, Bureau of Land Management

Out of crisis, innovation

Battling the fires of summer 2000 required unprecedented numbers of firefighters and tons of equipment. With both in short supply, national and regional fire-fighting managers had to pull off a monumental juggling act, moving supplies and personnel from one end of the country to another, often on an hour's notice. Among the myriad agencies responsible for this decision making was the Great Basin Multi-Agency Coordination (MAC) Group, which by early July was meeting twice a day—to assess the rapidly changing needs of incident commanders, and then moving always-insufficient resources where they were needed.

It was the toughest kind of decision making, not made any easier by the fact that much of the incoming information was in the form of written reports full of words and numbers and tables: as copy machines whirred endlessly, wildfires were destroying forests and homes and lives.

In late July, one of the MAC Group's members, veteran firefighter Robert Plantrich of the Bureau of Indian Affairs, sent off a memo urging the deployment of a new kind of tool, GIS, to help with some of the critical decision making. The response was astonishingly swift for a bureaucracy. Within hours, a conference call among GIS-savvy agencies was taking place, laying the groundwork for a national wildfire Web site.

Finding and allocating resources such as hand crews, planes, and vehicles was one of the toughest jobs of fire managers during the summer of 2000.

Photos courtesy of the Bureau of Land Management

One-stop fire shop

Within days of the conference call, the Geospatial Multi-Agency Coordination Group (GeoMAC) Web site was under construction on servers at the USGS Rocky Mountain Mapping Center in Colorado. The site would be a one-stop information shop, where fire-fighting managers could go for the latest information on fires. Many agencies had a voice in the site's development, notably the Forest Service and the Bureau of Land Management, on whose land many wildfires were burning. That meant there was a wealth of data that site developers from ESRI and USGS could work with. That wealth, in turn, dictated the technology that would be used—ArcIMS, the most up-to-date software for serving maps over the Internet, and ArcSDE™ for Oracle8i™ to harness all that data, with IBM® providing a server.

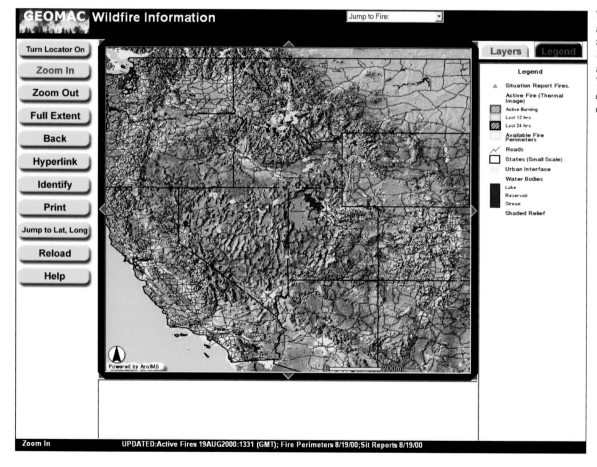

The GeoMAC Web site at the height of one of the worst wildfire seasons in U.S. history shows vividly the extent of the disaster. The green triangles show active but contained fires on August 19, 2000.

A satellite's-eye view

The GeoMAC site brings together real-time information—about the location and path of fires, as well as weather conditions—and combines it with basemaps that show fire managers in detail what kind of terrain and natural obstacles fire crews must contend with.

Green triangles indicate active fires reported from the field every morning and entered into a database maintained by the National Interagency Fire Center. From that, managers can get more detailed information via the Web about exactly how big the fire is, where it is, the number of people fighting it, the amount of damage it might end up causing, and possible causes.

Inset map can be turned on and off

Oregon/Idaho border

Pink indicates urban areas; white dots are towns

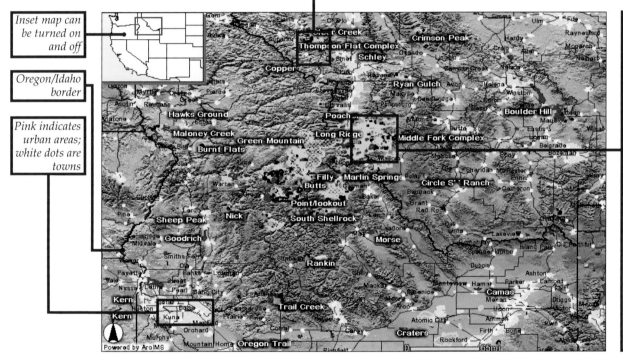

Red shapes delineate actively burning fires; orange, areas that burned within the previous 24 hours; and black, fires that burned 24 to 36 hours previously. This data comes from an infrared satellite that passes overhead and downlinks its information twice a day; sometimes it can show more about a fire's movements than people on the ground know, and can do so more quickly. The grey shapes indicate the perimeters of a fire as a whole, including previously burned areas.

This August view of the Idaho/Montana area shows how active the fire season was, and how much detail the public GeoMAC Web site could show. All the layers available on the public site have been turned on in this view.

A new view of destruction

The GeoMAC site came online just as a bad fire season got worse: at its height, a million acres were estimated to be on fire, with more than thirty thousand people working in fire-related jobs. Such extreme conditions required extreme strategies and tactics; in some places, larger fires were simply allowed to burn out so resources could be moved to smaller fires that posed a bigger threat, or that offered a better chance of suppression.

Since managers could now see—literally—the entire picture, sometimes better than could those on the ground, decisions were made with more confidence. For example, the GeoMAC site allowed them to see that a group of small fires was consolidating into one large fire, burning away from an urban area. Therefore, firefighters could be moved elsewhere.

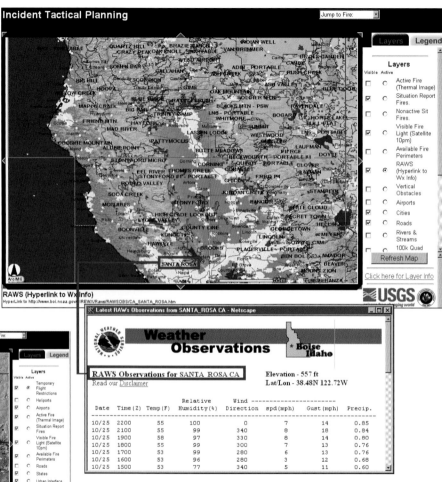

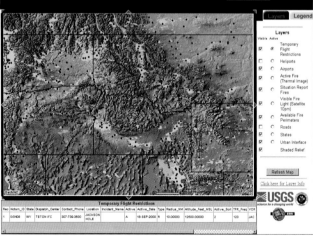

Members of the GeoMAC team can access additional resources and data layers at a nonpublic Web site. Above, clicking on a blue-dot hyperlink lets planners see real-time weather information from the National Weather Service, such as wind speed, wind direction, and humidity. The red grid indicates areas covered by available 1:250,000-scale USGS topographic maps. Wildfires and air traffic do not mix well, and the demonstration aviation site at the left shows how the locations of airports and restricted flight zones would be represented in a wildfire area.

Spreading the wealth and resources

GeoMAC is more than a Web site; it's an entirely new and powerful information resource for all firefighters, not just those at senior command levels.

Consolidating the GeoMAC data in one place has the additional benefit of giving commanders in the field—with flames roaring only a few feet away—an easier way to get the specific maps and data they need. Even though those commanders may not have the bandwidth to run the GeoMAC site at full throttle, its developers have set up data links that allow them, with a laptop and the right software, to download the specific data they need, even if it is from a database thousands of miles away, or from a satellite miles above the earth.

Think of it all as Pulaski, version 2.0.

The GeoMAC site is fueled by a broad array of government agencies providing a variety of data important in fire-fighting activities, all channeled through ArcSDE and ArcIMS software to the public and firefighters.

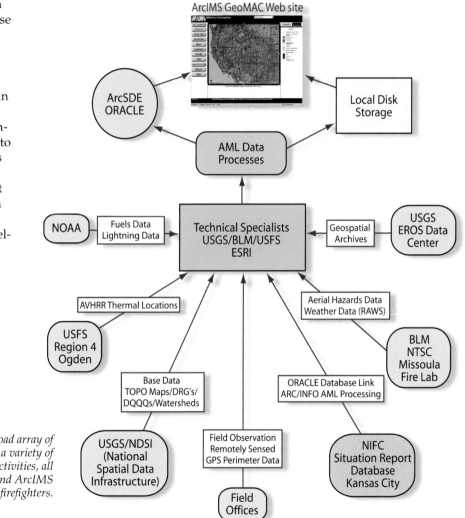

Acknowledgments

Thanks to Robert Plantrich, Bureau of Indian Affairs; John Guthrie and Dave Ozman of the U.S. Geological Survey; Jeff Baranyi and Tim Clark, ESRI–Denver; and Sheri Ascherfeld of the National Interagency Fire Center.

Web: wildfire.usgs.gov

Chapter 9

The Willow Incident: GPS and zero containment

THE EXACT NATURE OF ITS IGNITION is unknown, but the wildfire known as the Willow Incident began about 2:25 on the afternoon of August 28, 1999, just north of a resort community, Lake Arrowhead, in the San Bernardino National Forest. It escaped the attack of the first team on the scene, and the decision was made to bring in a National Incident Management Team. By ten that night, the fire had consumed thirty-two hundred acres.

By the morning of the 31st, about fifty thousand acres had burned. Two thousand people were working 114 engines, thirteen dozers, four helicopters, eighteen water tenders, and twenty retardant tankers. The gusting and erratic winds—direction shifting all over the compass—high temperatures, and low humidity that characterized the first days of the fire were forecast to continue. Three hundred more firefighters were called in. The unified command center was able to issue a statement to the effect that they had begun to contain the fire—perhaps as much as 20 percent of the blaze was under some kind of control.

Investigation of the Willow Incident, one of the biggest single fires in California history, points to a human cause, either arson or carelessness. All the conditions were right for an out-of-control blaze.

Day six: turning the corner

On the morning of September 2, that figure was revised to 35 percent. Crews continued to burn out fuels between fire-lines and blackened areas, while helicopters and air tankers dropped water on hot spots. The fire was making no runs into new areas, and more stable weather was taking over. Something like three million dollars had been spent so far.

After six days and $3 million, the fire was one-third contained.

Fifty-percent containment was reached the following day. Firefighters were chipping ice off their tents in the morning, but the cooler temps and calmer winds were more than welcome. One-hundred-percent containment was in sight. The number of acres burned at that point was estimated at 61,770. The next day's estimate was 62,820. The fire had a ninety-mile-long perimeter and was 80 percent contained. The hard and dirty work of mopping up began: making sure that no sparks caught fuel within four hundred feet of the fire line.

Smoke was still visible as the interior of the fire burned itself out, but full containment was announced on September 5.

Willow Incident August 31 11:30 a.m.

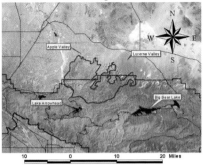

Willow Incident September 1, 12:00 p.m.

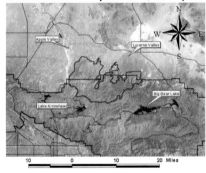

Willow Incident September 2, 12:00 p.m.

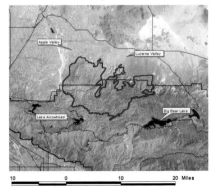

A GPS receiver, a laptop, and a helicopter were used to establish the fire's perimeter as it grew.

Flaming fronts and fire lines

A fire that big moving that fast calls for indirect tactics: containment lines are built with axes, chainsaws, shovels, and dozers, using existing roads and trails when possible. The fire is either allowed to burn from its flaming front to the containment lines, or firefighters "burn out" from containment lines to flaming front, thereby eliminating flammable vegetation.

Firefighters burning out an area between the front of the fire and a containment line.

Large wildfires also call for a lot of information to be gathered and made useful in a very short period of time. The direction or directions the fire is heading, the directions it might take—and just as importantly, why—the locations of crews, equipment, structures, and people in the path or potential path of the fire— these things are extremely hard to keep clear when the area in question is so vast and the data changing so quickly.

Finding and using data pertinent to fighting the fire isn't the only job, however, that the command center is faced with. As the number of structures, homes, and businesses increases in areas where the risk of wildfire is great, the more the people concerned want to know about what's being done to protect their property, and why.

Decisions about where tankers should drop retardant, where fire lines should be built, and where other tactics might be effective, can only be made properly when the information is accurate and timely.

100-percent explainment

Tom Patterson works for the National
Park Service and has his office in Joshua
Tree National Park. He was part of a tactical GIS mapping team composed of GIS
specialists from the California Governor's Office of Emergency Services, Kern
County Fire Department, and Marin
County Fire Department. His job was to
put on a helmet, strap a rather heavy and
cumbersome laptop around his middle—
a little bit like the way folksingers strap
harmonicas around their necks—get in
one of the four helicopters, and fly the
fire's perimeter.

Using a hand-held GPS (Global Positioning System) receiver using military
Y-code radio signals transmitted by satel-
lites to take extremely accurate latitude
and longitude measurements, Patterson
took readings as fast as he could, entering
the coordinates into ArcView GIS on the
laptop via GPS data-conversion software.

*GPS-generated latitude/longitude
coordinates can quickly and easily
become a 3-D model, or be laid
over existing maps.*

Once the data was in place, he was able to draw the changing shape of the fire on any number of map backgrounds or thematic displays: fuel and slope models, structure location and density, road networks, crew deployment, hot spots, blackened areas, containment lines—all this was more or less instantly available to anyone who needed to know within the unified command, no matter where they happened to be, and was updated regularly—anytime Patterson could find a pilot.

Better still, he could make presentations to the media, representatives of local governments, and concerned citizens that clearly and vividly illustrated the nature and movement of the fire. He could explain why the fire was behaving as it was, predict where it was headed and what it would do when it got there, and justify the decisions the command was making about tactics: where the lines would be drawn, what areas would be left to burn, and so on.

In other words, it was information that went two ways: into the hands of firefighters struggling to surround a fire sixty-five-thousand acres big, and into the heads of people who would foot the bill, and whose homes and livelihoods lay in harm's way.

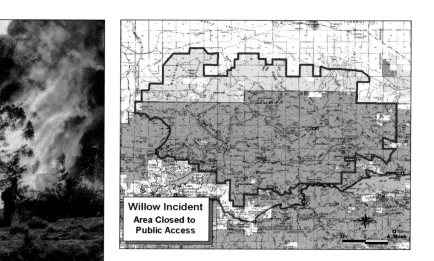

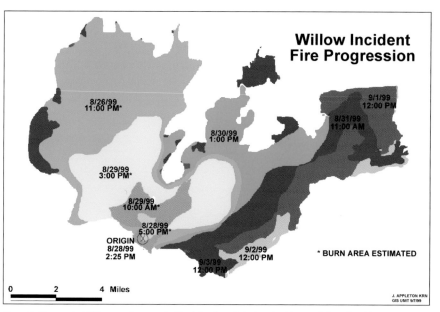

Tom Patterson's GIS mapping made the job of explaining tactics and the situation— often one of the hardest parts of the job—much easier.

Acknowledgments

Special thanks to Tom Patterson, fire management officer, National Park Service.

E-mail: Tom_Patterson@nps.gov

Ouachita Civil Defense Agency: Project Impact and the disaster-resistant community

THE FEDERAL EMERGENCY MANAGEMENT AGENCY spent twenty-five billion dollars during the 1990s, repairing homes, businesses, and communities damaged by natural disasters. That's a two-and-a-half-billion-a-year tab for picking up the pieces—which doesn't include insurance claims (also in the billions), lost revenue and jobs, and funds coming from elsewhere in the government.

Looking for ways to prune that figure back, FEMA came up with Project Impact: Building Disaster-Resistant Communities. Pilot programs in seven communities around the country commenced in late 1997, and went over so well that there are now more than 250 communities participating, with business partners numbering in the thousands.

Project Impact operates according to three principles: preventive actions must be decided at the local level; private-sector participation is vital; and long-term efforts and investments in prevention measures are essential. FEMA offers expertise and technical assistance from the national and regional level and includes other federal agencies and states in the equation.

Ouachita Parish in Louisiana is a Project Impact Star Community, one of eleven awarded grants in November of 2000, at Project Impact's Summit 2000. Ouachita is also the recipient of an ESRI Local Government Start-up Grant. The two grants have helped the parish, and particularly its civil defense agency, back up its practical knowledge and experience with the development and implementation of GIS technology.

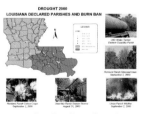

Drought, flooding, hurricanes, tornadoes, wildfires, and chemical and oil spills regularly assail Louisiana. Ouachita Parish, in the north central part of the state, has received several awards for its GIS-driven emergency preparedness planning.

Froggy Bottom

The Froggy Bottom community is located in eastern Ouachita Parish. It is inundated or threatened with inundation annually. Flooding caused evacuation of the community in the winter of 1999 and the spring of 2000.

As if that weren't enough, a combination of drought and increased agricultural activity caused the area's aquifer to drop below the depth of homeowner water wells in the community: too much water above ground and not enough below. In July 2000, a state of emergency was declared in order to receive state assistance. The Louisiana Office of Emergency Preparedness provided a Louisiana National Guard five-thousand-gallon water tanker. Tom Malmay, director of the Ouachita Civil Defense Agency (OCDA), responded with the GIS-driven "Froggy Bottom Action Plan."

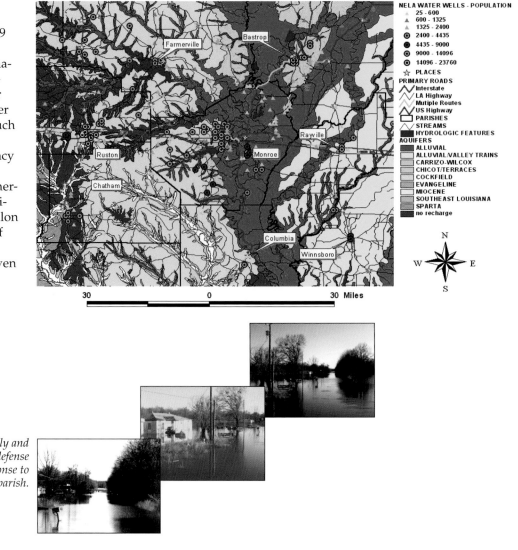

NORTHEAST LOUISIANA WATER WELLS AND AQUIFERS
WMD Program

NELA WATER WELLS - POPULATION
- 25 - 600
- 600 - 1325
- 1325 - 2400
- 2400 - 4435
- 4435 - 9000
- 9000 - 14096
- 14096 - 23760
- ☆ PLACES

PRIMARY ROADS
- Interstate
- LA Highway
- Mutiple Routes
- US Highway
- PARISHES
- STREAMS
- HYDROLOGIC FEATURES

AQUIFERS
- ALLUVIAL
- ALLUVIAL/VALLEY TRAINS
- CARRIZO-WILCOX
- CHICOT/TERRACES
- COCKFIELD
- EVANGELINE
- MIOCENE
- SOUTHEAST LOUISIANA
- SPARTA
- no recharge

30   0   30   Miles

Comprehensive data dealing with water supply and use is an important part of the parish's civil defense database. It figured prominently in the response to flooding in the eastern parish.

The action plan

Eleven homes were targeted for removal from the flood hazard area, the first five to be bought out by the last day of December 2000, the remaining six families to be relocated by the middle of April 2001.

The low aquifer put the water supply of fourteen other families in jeopardy. A local state of emergency was declared and a request made for the Louisiana National Guard to bring in a five-thousand-gallon water tanker, to remain on site until April 2001. The Louisiana National Guard also developed a winter weather program for tanker use. The American Red Cross was ready to help with the provision of potable water in the event the LNG had to pull the tanker for use elsewhere.

The City of Monroe, Ouachita Parish Police Jury, and Greater Ouachita Water agreed in principle to a plan to provide water to eastern Ouachita Parish. The plan includes running water lines to the relocated homes. Homes not targeted for acquisition or relocation but affected by the low aquifer may also use these water lines.

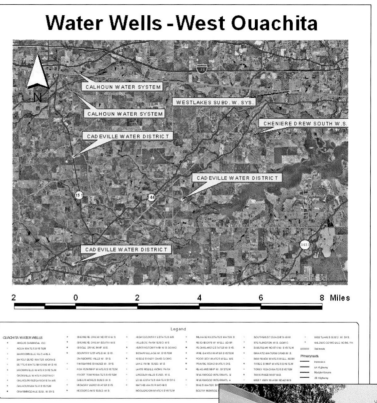

Wells in western Ouachita Parish had to supply the eastern reaches of the parish as well, which were suffering floods and drought at the same time. The Louisiana National Guard supplied and operated a water tanker.

Girl Scouts and the Preparedness Fair

The FEMA seed grant funds have been put to use building partnerships with local businesses and organizations. One of the most unique, interesting, and effective programs came about over a phone call between Malmay and Gail Collins, a Girl Scout troop leader. The idea of a preparedness fair quickly emerged as one full of possibilities for community engagement. On August 5, 2000, the scouts, with the aid of twenty local organizations, set up booths, each dealing with a different aspect of disaster preparedness: How Water is Contaminated, School Violence, The First Responder's Responsibilities, The Homeless in a Disaster, Taking Care of Pets in a Disaster, Wildlife and Their Habitat in a Disaster, The Elderly in an Emergency, and many more.

**POPULATION DENSITY DISPLAY
AGE GROUP 65 AND UP**

The Girl Scouts and the Ouachita Civil Defense Agency came together in a Preparedness Fair, featuring booths staffed with scouts and representatives of numerous community organizations, dispensing valuable information about how to prepare for and deal with disasters and emergencies.

Tornadoes

The Gulf Stream, as it migrates north in the spring with hot, moist air, and south in the fall with cold, dry air, brings two seasons of severe weather to Louisiana, which ranks eleventh in states on the all-time tornado hit list. These storms have caused hundreds of millions of dollars of damage and killed hundreds of people. Faced with destructive power of that magnitude, dropping out of the sky with almost no warning, death and injury seem unavoidable—but the fact is that tornado preparedness saves lives.

An informed public, practiced in the ways of seeking shelter in a sudden emergency, is central to tornado preparedness, and to that end the OCDA planned and promoted the "Fall 2000 Tornado Drill."

One school was chosen to demonstrate the drill. Emergency responders, including representatives from the Louisiana Office of Emergency Preparedness, police and fire departments, ARES (Amateur Radio Emergency Service), Red Cross, and the media, were present to observe and evaluate the students' response.

The centerpiece of a campaign to raise awareness, the Fall 2000 Tornado Drill served to make clear the connection between information and active response that GIS can help to foster.

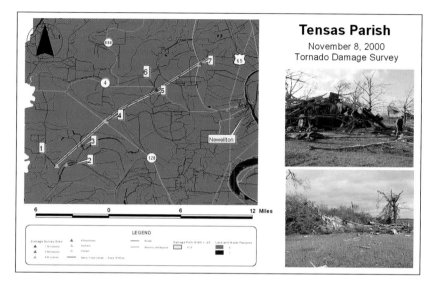

Tensas Parish
November 8, 2000
Tornado Damage Survey

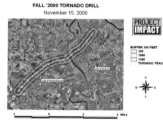

FALL '2000 TORNADO DRILL
November 15, 2000

Understanding the behavior of tornadoes is an important part of knowing how to survive them.

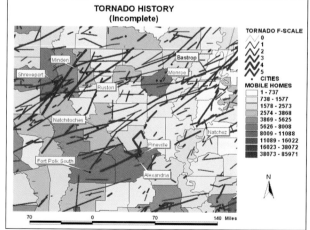

TORNADO HISTORY
(Incomplete)

HAZMAT spills

Given the high profile and intense activity of the petroleum-refining industry in Louisiana, the storage and transportation of hazardous materials (HAZMAT) has become as great a potential threat to public safety as the unpredictable forces of nature. An accident on the highway can become a matter of serious concern for a whole community if the vehicle happens to be carrying toxic chemicals, for instance.

Part of the OCDA's mission is to establish incident command posts in such cases, and to function as a multiported clearinghouse and conduit of information for other responding agencies.

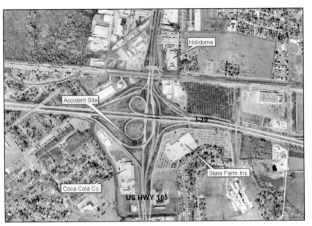

A motor carrier transporting hazardous materials overturned at the intersection of an interstate highway and a U.S. highway, in the middle of Ouachita Parish. The OCDA established a command post, briefed numerous other agencies and the media, and provided food and water as well.

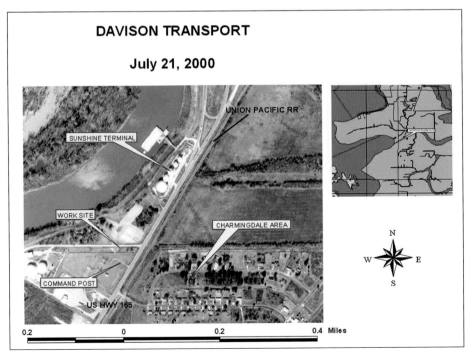

Ice storms

Louisiana, with the Gulf of Mexico, swamps, bayous, alligators, and hot, humid weather, isn't the first place you might think of when it comes to ice storms, but its position in a border region between temperate and subtropical climate zones makes for unlikely and unpredictable possibilities—if not a tornado, then an ice storm, which can shut whole states down when conditions are right.

In the event of such an emergency, accurate information about quickly changing conditions is vital: the location of sanding trucks, accidents, downed power lines, fallen trees, temperature shifts, microclimates, and so on. This kind of knowledge can make the difference between a hundred-car smashup and an empty, icy road, slowly melting.

This map shows parishes under an ice storm warning, ramped according to population.

Acknowledgments

Thanks to Tom Malmay, director,
Ouachita Civil Defense Agency.

E-mail: civil@bayou.com

Chapter 11

Los Angeles County Fire Department: Hospital closed!

WHAT'S THE FIRST THING that comes to mind when you think of Los Angeles? Hollywood and the movies? Probably, but heavy traffic has got to be somewhere near the top. Veteran Angeleno drivers refer to two kinds of traffic: bad and surreal.

Fire trucks and ambulances have lights and sirens, of course, and other motorists generally try to get out of the way of emergency vehicles, but reducing response times—a critical endeavor no matter where your area of service is—can be especially onerous in vast and traffic-jammed Los Angeles County.

Complicate that scenario by closing a hospital and you get an idea what the Los Angeles County Fire Department was up against.

Battalion Five Squad Study

In the northern reaches of Battalion Five's area of service (AOS), where Ventura and Los Angeles counties meet, only one hospital, the Westlake, had the facilities to handle Emergency Medical Service (EMS).

It closed.

Shutting down Westlake Hospital meant that Los Robles Hospital, across the line in Ventura County, would have to handle EMS for a much larger, out-of-county, area. It also meant that transport times from deep inside Battalion Five's AOS would be substantially increased. "Out-of-service" time would increase as well for the sole squad in the area.

The Los Angeles County Fire Department decided to study response times in the Battalion Five district. Using ARC/INFO, the GIS Section of the department's Information Management Division was asked to create and analyze several different scenarios for new schemes of service in the old Westlake area. Based on that analysis, it was asked to conclude the project with a recommendation.

The maps on the next pages illustrate that decision-making process step by step. All of the maps show response times averaged across three squads—the 125th, the 71st, and the 88th—weighted by linear street mileage.

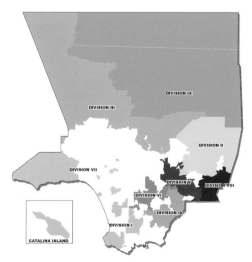

Hospital still in business

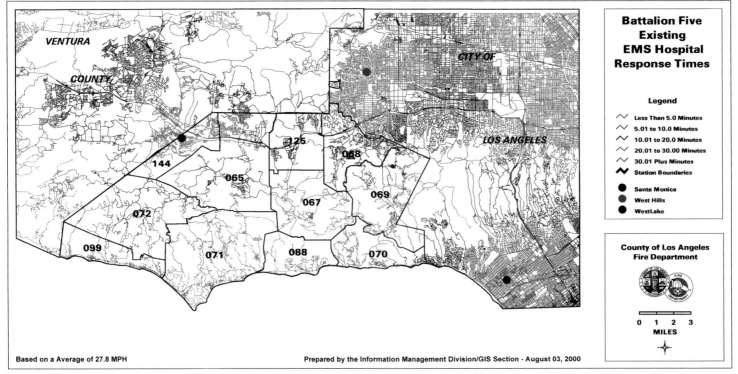

This map shows response times to the three Emergency Medical Service hospitals, as they existed before the closing of Westlake.

Hospital out of business

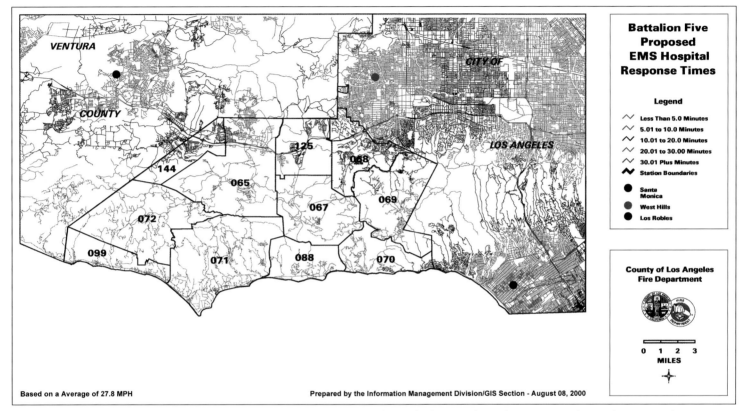

When Westlake closed, Los Robles in Ventura County became the closest EMS hospital. This map shows the consequent changes in response times.

Fire season

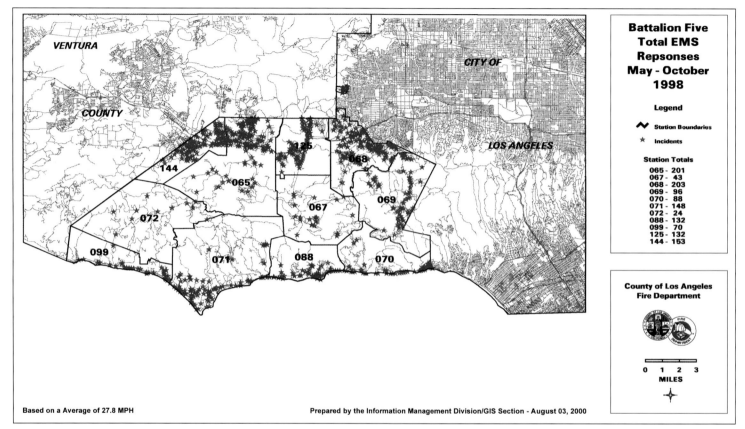

Response times change seasonally. This map is of the busiest part of the year, May to October.

Hospital closed and one squad down

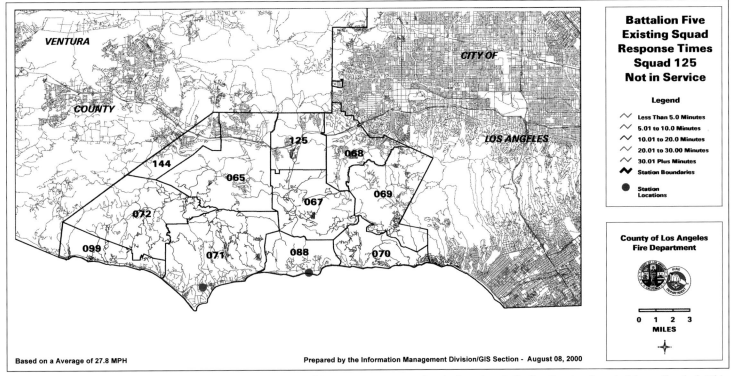

When one squad is out of service (a period of necessary downtime following a response and arrival at a hospital), the other two have to take up the slack. This map shows that if the 125th was out of service in the northern part of the area, it would take the 71st and the 88th more than twenty minutes to respond.

A different squad down

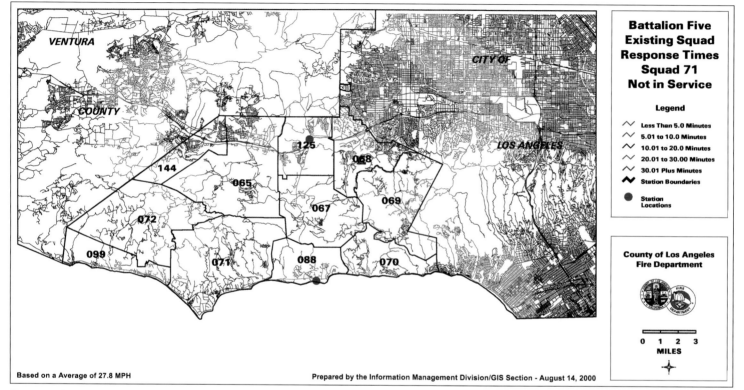

Response times when the 71st is out of service.

The last squad down

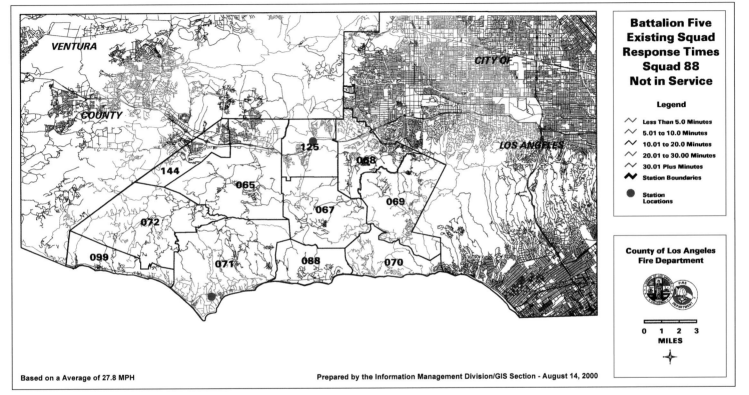

Response times when the 88th is out of service.

Scenario number one

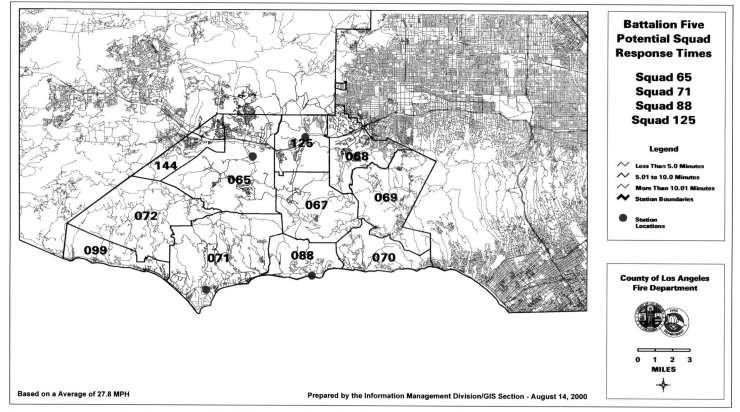

One scenario: response times if a new squad, the 65th, were put in service with the other three in their current locations.

Scenario number two

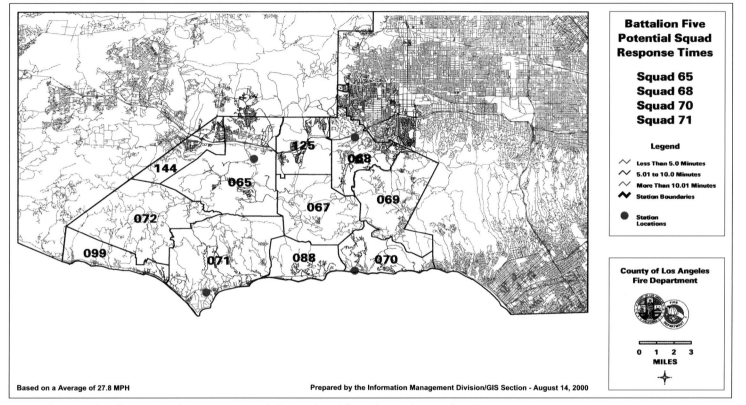

A second scenario has the new squad at Station 65, with the 125th and the 88th moved to new locations.

The winner: Scenario number three

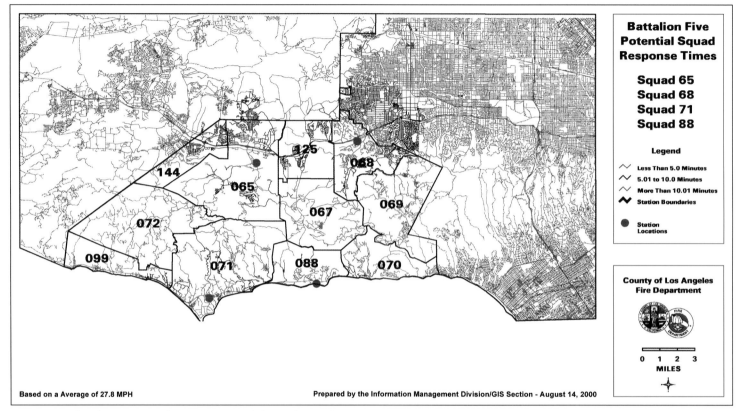

Scenario number three: new squad at Station 65, and the 125th moved to Station 68. This deployment provided the best coverage possible, and eliminated the out-of-service problem in the northern part of Battalion Five's district. Using actual response times and GIS, the battalion was able to simulate the real world and arrive at decisions that made the best of what it had to deal with.

Counting seconds

The loss of a hospital is a major blow to a community. The problems of where to send people and how to get them there are problems on which lives depend. Add to that sense of urgency the number of variables involved in planning a solution, especially in a heavily populated and complex urban landscape like Los Angeles County, and you have one of the most serious and complicated projects a municipality can undertake. By using GIS, the LACFD was able to sort through a vast amount of data, make quick analyses of a variety of scenarios, and illustrate clear consequences of each plan. To say the Battalion Five Squad Study is a success story is to put it mildly. When seconds count, those seconds have to be counted—every plan becomes guesswork otherwise.

Acknowledgments

Thanks to Tim Smith at the Los Angeles County Fire Department.

Web: fire.co.la.ca.us

Chapter 12

The Northridge quake: Picking up the pieces

LOS ANGELES, January 17, 1994, 4:31 in the morning: a few seconds of geologic convulsion killed at least fifty-six people, injured seven thousand more, and left twenty thousand people homeless. Three-quarters of a million insurance claims were filed, and about forty billion dollars' worth of damage was done.

Millions of tons of debris had to be hauled off and put somewhere else. Shelters had to be built, food and water supplied, damaged buildings inspected, rebuilt, or torn down. Ruptured lines of transportation and power had to be restored. The vast but delicate web that makes living possible in Southern California—by nearly all measures an uninhabitable region—had to be carefully threaded back together.

It was back-breaking, mind-bending labor, involving individuals, organizations, and institutions from every walk, level, and sector of American society. The coordination of these efforts could have been a nightmare of aggravated hardship, frustration, and misapplied resources.

The Northridge earthquake measured 6.7 on the Richter scale. Quakes of greater magnitude, like the 7.1 Hector Mine temblor in 1999, can cause much less damage if they are centered far from dense populations. Northridge is part of metropolitan Los Angeles.

California Governor's Office of Emergency Services

Established in 1950, and working under its present name since California's adoption of the Emergency Services Act in 1970, the state Office of Emergency Services (OES) receives and processes requests from local organizations responding to a disaster or large-scale emergency, and coordinates those responses.

The OES Warning Center is staffed around the clock and every day of the year. Controllers speak every day with county OES offices, and with the National Warning Center in Berryville, Virginia. A toxic spill hotline is maintained, along with the state's Urban Search and Rescue, Safety Assessment Volunteer, and Telecommunications Mutual Aid programs.

In an emergency, the OES can call on any and all state agencies for advice and support. The California National Guard, the Highway Patrol, the departments of Forestry and Fire Protection, Social Services, Health Services, and Transportation, and the Conservation Corps are most often called upon.

The Northridge earthquake was a baptism of fire for GIS operations, which were slowly being developed when the quake happened.

OES and GIS

The OES began working GIS into its tactical operations in 1990 as part of a program for nuclear power preparedness. Hardware, software, and data were rolled over from Nuclear Power Preparedness (NPP) exercises for use elsewhere—in a flood or riot, for example—then improved and rolled back for another NPP exercise. The GIS staff grew, the computers got faster, the networks more inclusive, the data more complete.

Then the firestorms of 1993 hit, causing several billion dollars' worth of damage. Rapid set-up techniques learned in the NPP exercises were combined with new Global Positioning System technology to quickly map all eighteen fire perimeters. Working with FEMA, OES set up three application centers to speed up the damage relief process, and each of the centers featured GIS staff and equipment.

The nucleus of the kind of GIS operation that would be able to handle a major disaster was in place—just in time for Northridge.

The Northridge earthquake GIS operation had to be developed on the fly, but proved successful, thanks in part to exercises performed for California's Nuclear Power Preparedness program and experience with the firestorms of '93.

True adventure

David Kehrlein woke early on Martin Luther King, Jr. Day, poured himself a cup of coffee, and got ready to do some shopping with his wife. He was looking forward to a little free time after intensive work on the recent firestorms, but was stopped in his tracks, cup halfway to his mouth, by what he was seeing on TV: collapsed freeway overpasses, apartment houses broken in two, toppled buildings, chaos.

He saw quite clearly that his life was going to change, but had no idea how big the Northridge earthquake GIS project would turn out to be, how much time and energy would be swallowed up, how stressful it would become.

Arriving in Pasadena, Kehrlein sat down with Terrie Monaghan of the OES Southern Region, Hurricane Andrew veteran Tom Muhol, and FEMA's Dan Cotter to hash out the architecture of a bigger and better GIS. The first task was to put emergency housing grant applications on a fast track. Applicants automatically qualified for assistance if their ZIP Codes were within a zone valued at 8 or higher on a Modified Mercalli Shaking Intensity map.

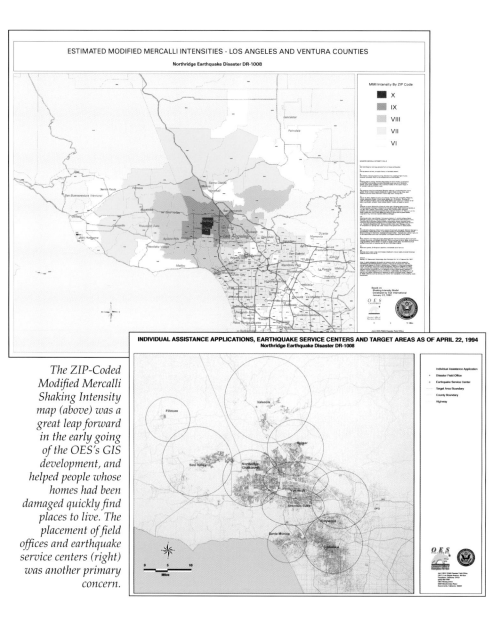

The ZIP-Coded Modified Mercalli Shaking Intensity map (above) was a great leap forward in the early going of the OES's GIS development, and helped people whose homes had been damaged quickly find places to live. The placement of field offices and earthquake service centers (right) was another primary concern.

Structure stoplights

The team started with three computers and one HP® 650C plotter. They had two hundred square feet of space, in one corner of a larger room, and Kehrlein's desk was a big blue footlocker. They worked sixteen to eighteen hours a day, moving on from emergency housing applications to a classification scheme based on damage data coming out of the City of Los Angeles (within the boundaries of which 80 percent of the destruction had occurred). Structures were ranked noninhabitable, habitable at your own risk, and habitable at no risk—red, yellow, or green, respectively, on GIS maps that integrated the danger ranking with the number of teams in the field, their locations, and the availability of interpreters in areas where English was a second language.

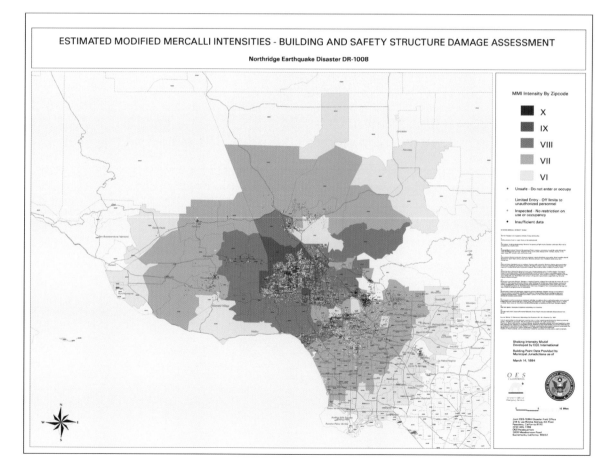

Red, green, and yellow color-coded ranking of structures in the greater Los Angeles area shows where the greatest numbers of uninhabitable and potentially dangerous buildings were. The ranking helped relief organizations deploy resources more effectively.

Bigger space and more people

After the first week, the operation doubled in size and staff: the California Department of Forestry sent two more people down, and floor space expanded to four hundred square feet. Kehrlein got a real desk. More importantly, they began to beef up their hardware, with first-generation Pentium®-based PCs, two SPARC™ 20s, a SPARC 10, a dual-processor SPARCserver™ 1000, and a Novell® server. It took one staff member ten sixteen-hour days to requisition, order, and arrange for the equipment to be delivered, but it was worth it, as more and better maps began to flow out the door. The goal was to create two identical sets of data, one on the PC side of their house, focused on maps for operations, and one on the UNIX side for higher-end analysis.

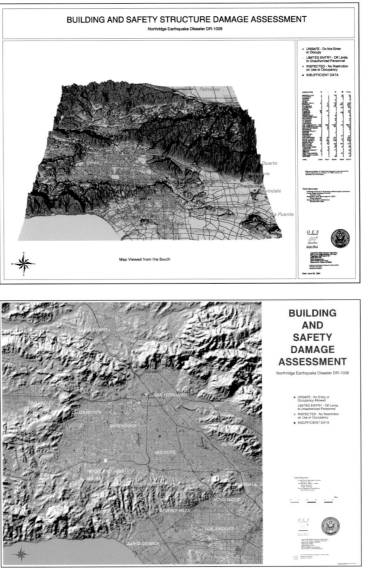

As office space, staff, and hardware capacities increased, so did the sophistication of the maps the GIS team was able to produce. These show two different 3-D views of the general patterns of structure damage.

Growing pains and puzzle pieces

The GIS team continued to work at a feverish pace, but one aspect of the project became more troublesome as the days went by: analysis of operational requirements. This is a hard enough task under normal circumstances; in the wake of an earthquake, learning and inventing new capabilities as you go—it's almost impossible. Kehrlein put it this way:

"How do you get good feedback when you ask someone how much of something, that they've never used or even seen before, would they use if they could have it? They really have no way of knowing, even if they understand what you're talking about."

They turned to the organizational chart developed by the Hurricane Andrew GIS staff, and tried to match it with the functions they believed most necessary at that point. They came up with twice the number of positions figured on at the outset, and began an effort to increase staff to fifteen analysts, five support workers, and three managers.

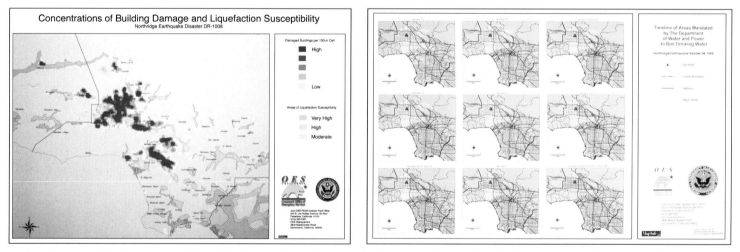

Coping with uncertainties over what information to provide and how to go about creating those products, the GIS team nevertheless managed to make maps covering a wide spectrum of information. The map at the left compares degree of building damage and the area's susceptibility to liquefaction (a geological process that turns land to mush and sets up particularly destructive wave-like action). The map at the right charts the safety and changing conditions of the water supply: where water had to be boiled on a day-to-day basis.

The final shape of things

There was not, in early 1994, a surplus of GIS experts—or even apprentices. Recruiting mainly through universities— a flyer was faxed to a number of schools and departments calling for applicants wishing to be "masters of disaster"—and relying on references supplied by people they hired first, the OES GIS team ended up with four experienced users and about ten highly motivated beginners.

There was no standardized directory, nor a complete network, so newcomers had to hunt for the data they needed to do their jobs. Only data set-up people knew where most of the data could be found, and analysts knew only as much as they needed to know. Battling with FEMA space managers, the team acquired first 1,100 square feet and finally 1,900. The team was divided into three sections: ARC/INFO analysts, data managers, and PC map producers. Gradually, day by day, the GIS operation cleaned itself up and hit its stride.

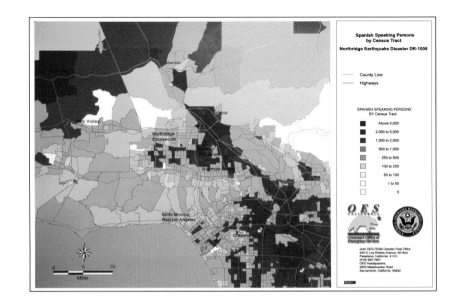

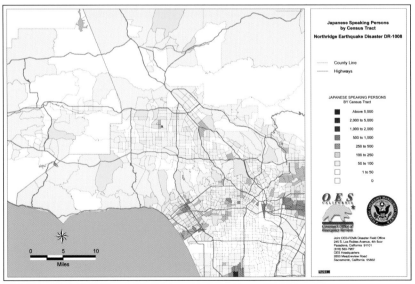

Management of chaos inside the GIS operation and on the ruined streets of Los Angeles depended on the speedy and accurate interpretation of information. These two maps illustrate one small example: where to put Japanese- and Spanish-speaking interpreters.

In retrospect

"It was a very intense operation," Kehrlein says. "People always remarked about the electricity in the air when they walked into the room. The GIS folks were always glued to their screens, putting the final touches on their latest masterpieces. After a few months, the mental health folks were seriously concerned about us, because the workload was still high, the hours were still at ten to twelve a day, six days a week, and folks were very focused. This seriously creeped out the touchy-feely types."

It was in many respects breakthrough work in the use of GIS in disaster response and management. Budget levels remained cloudy, though a million dollars seemed possible, and the drawing up of contracts created a good deal of anxiety as Kehrlein tried to figure out how to bring outside contractors on board to actually do the things the team wanted to do.

"The technique I used," says Kehrlein, "was to muddle forward." Modest as that sounds, an awful lot of ruptured earth was covered in just that way.

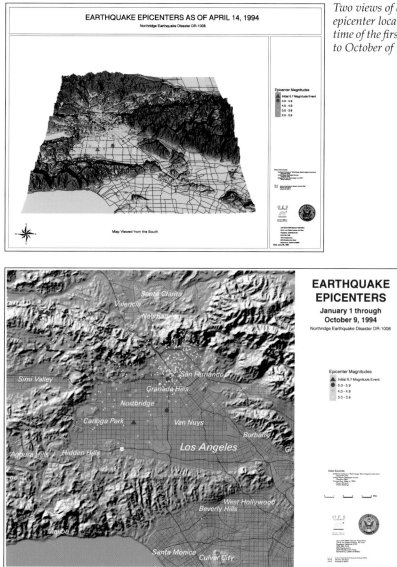

Two views of earthquake epicenter locations from the time of the first Northridge blast to October of the same year.

Acknowledgments

Thanks to David Kehrlein and Kris Higgs at the California Governor's Office of Emergency Services.

Web: www.oes.ca.gov

GIScience

GIS for Everyone SECOND EDITION
Now everyone can create smart maps for school, work, home, or community action using a personal computer. This revised second edition includes the ArcExplorer™ geographic data viewer and more than 500 megabytes of geographic data. ISBN 1-879102-91-9 196 pages

The ESRI Guide to GIS Analysis, Volume 1: Geographic Patterns and Relationships
An important new book about how to do real analysis with a geographic information system. *The ESRI Guide to GIS Analysis* focuses on six of the most common geographic analysis tasks. ISBN 1-879102-06-4 188 pages

Modeling Our World: The ESRI Guide to Geodatabase Design
With this comprehensive guide and reference to GIS data modeling and to the new geodatabase model introduced with ArcInfo™ 8, you'll learn how to make the right decisions about modeling data, from database design and data capture to spatial analysis and visual presentation. ISBN 1-879102-62-5 216 pages

Hydrologic and Hydraulic Modeling Support with Geographic Information Systems
This book presents the invited papers in water resources at the 1999 ESRI International User Conference. Covering practical issues related to hydrologic and hydraulic water quantity modeling support using GIS, the concepts and techniques apply to any hydrologic and hydraulic model requiring spatial data or spatial visualization.
ISBN 1-879102-80-3 232 pages

Beyond Maps: GIS and Decision Making in Local Government
Beyond Maps shows how local governments are making geographic information systems true management tools. Packed with real-life examples, it explores innovative ways to use GIS to improve local government operations. ISBN 1-879102-79-X 240 pages

The ESRI Press Dictionary of GIS Terminology
This long-needed and authoritative reference brings together the language and nomenclature of the many GIS-related disciplines and applications. Designed for students, professionals, researchers, and technicians, the dictionary provides succinct and accurate definitions of more than a thousand terms. ISBN 1-879102-78-1 128 pages

Planning Support Systems: Integrating Geographic Information Systems, Models, and Visualization Tools
Richard Brail of Rutgers University's Edward J. Bloustein School of Planning and Public Policy, and Richard Klosterman of the University of Akron, have assembled papers from colleagues around the globe who are working to expand the applicability and understanding of the top issues in computer-aided planning. ISBN 1-58948-011-2 468 pages

Geographic Information Systems and Science
This comprehensive guide to GIS, geographic information science (GIScience), and GIS management illuminates some shared concerns of business, government, and science. It looks at how issues of management, ethics, risk, and technology intersect, and at how GIS provides a gateway to problem solving, and links to special learning modules at ESRI® Virtual Campus (campus.esri.com). ISBN 0-471-89275-0 472 pages

Mapping Census 2000: The Geography of U.S. Diversity
Cartographers Cynthia A. Brewer and Trudy A. Suchan have taken Census 2000 data and assembled an atlas of maps that illustrates the new American diversity in rich and vivid detail. The result is an atlas of America and of Americans that is notable both for its comprehensiveness and for its precision. ISBN 1-58948-014-7 120 pages

Undersea with GIS
Explore how GIS is illuminating the mysteries hidden in the earth's oceans. Leading-edge applications include managing protected underwater sanctuaries, tracking whale migration, and recent advances in the development of 3-D electronic navigational charts. Companion CD–ROM brings the underwater world to life for both the undersea practitioner and student and includes 3-D underwater flythroughs, ArcView® extensions for marine applications, a K–12 lesson plan, and more. ISBN 1-58948-016-3 276 pages

My Community, Our Earth: A Student Project Guide to Sustainable Development and Geography
Get students involved in an international project about important ideas and practical applications for sustainable development. This book provides guidelines and resources to create a project that could be selected to be on display at the World Summit on Sustainable Development in South Africa in September 2002. For high-school and college students. ISBN 1-58948-039-2 132 pages

CONTINUED ON NEXT PAGE

Other books from **ESRI Press** *continued*

GIScience continued

Past Time, Past Place: GIS for History
In this pioneering book that encompasses the Greek and Roman eras, the Salem witch trials, the Dust Bowl of the 1930s, and more, leading scholars explain how GIS technology can illuminate the study of history. Richly illustrated, *Past Time, Past Place* is a vivid supplement to many courses in cultural studies and will fascinate armchair historians. ISBN 1-58948-032-5 224 pages

Mapping Our World: GIS Lessons for Educators
A comprehensive educational resource that gives any teacher all the tools needed to begin teaching GIS technology in the middle- or high-school classroom. Includes nineteen complete GIS lesson plans, a one-year license of ArcView 3.x, geographic data, a teacher resource CD, and a companion Web site. ISBN 1-58948-022-8 564 pages

ESRI Map Book, Volume 16: Geography—Creating Communities
A full-color collection of some of the finest maps produced using GIS software. Published annually since 1984, this unique book celebrates the mapping achievements of GIS professionals. *Directions Magazine* (www.directionsmag.com) has called the *ESRI Map Book* "The best map book in print." ISBN 1-58948-015-5 120 pages

The Case Studies Series

ArcView GIS Means Business
Written for business professionals, this book is a behind-the-scenes look at how some of America's most successful companies have used desktop GIS technology. The book is loaded with full-color illustrations and comes with a trial copy of ArcView software and a GIS tutorial. ISBN 1-879102-51-X 136 pages

Zeroing In: Geographic Information Systems at Work in the Community
In twelve "tales from the digital map age," this book shows how people use GIS in their daily jobs. An accessible and engaging introduction to GIS for anyone who deals with geographic information. ISBN 1-879102-50-1 128 pages

Serving Maps on the Internet
Take an insider's look at how today's forward-thinking organizations distribute map-based information via the Internet. Case studies cover a range of applications for ArcView Internet Map Server technology from ESRI. This book should interest anyone who wants to publish geospatial data on the World Wide Web. ISBN 1-879102-52-8 144 pages

Managing Natural Resources with GIS
Find out how GIS technology helps people design solutions to such pressing challenges as wildfires, urban blight, air and water degradation, species endangerment, disaster mitigation, coastline erosion, and public education. The experiences of public and private organizations provide real-world examples. ISBN 1-879102-53-6 132 pages

Enterprise GIS for Energy Companies
A volume of case studies showing how electric and gas utilities use geographic information systems to manage their facilities more cost effectively, find new market opportunities, and better serve their customers. ISBN 1-879102-48-X 120 pages

Transportation GIS
From monitoring rail systems and airplane noise levels, to making bus routes more efficient and improving roads, this book describes how geographic information systems have emerged as the tool of choice for transportation planners. ISBN 1-879102-47-1 132 pages

GIS for Landscape Architects

From Karen Hanna, noted landscape architect and GIS pioneer, comes *GIS for Landscape Architects*. Through actual examples, you'll learn how landscape architects, land planners, and designers now rely on GIS to create visual frameworks within which spatial data and information are gathered, interpreted, manipulated, and shared. ISBN 1-879102-64-1 120 pages

GIS for Health Organizations

Health management is a rapidly developing field, where even slight shifts in policy affect the health care we receive. In this book, you'll see how physicians, public health officials, insurance providers, hospitals, epidemiologists, researchers, and HMO executives use GIS to focus resources to meet the needs of those in their care. ISBN 1-879102-65-X 112 pages

GIS in Public Policy: Using Geographic Information for More Effective Government

This book shows how policy makers and others on the front lines of public service are putting GIS to work—to carry out the will of voters and legislators, and to inform and influence their decisions. *GIS in Public Policy* shows vividly the very real benefits of this new digital tool for anyone with an interest in, or influence over, the ways our institutions shape our lives. ISBN 1-879102-66-8 120 pages

Integrating GIS and the Global Positioning System

The Global Positioning System is an explosively growing technology. *Integrating GIS and the Global Positioning System* covers the basics of GPS and presents several case studies that illustrate some of the ways the power of GPS is being harnessed to GIS, ensuring, among other benefits, increased accuracy in measurement and completeness of coverage. ISBN 1-879102-81-1 112 pages

GIS in Schools

GIS is transforming classrooms—and learning—in elementary, middle, and high schools across North America. *GIS in Schools* documents what happens when students are exposed to GIS. The book gives teachers practical ideas about how to implement GIS in the classroom, and some theory behind the success stories. ISBN 1-879102-85-4 128 pages

Disaster Response: GIS for Public Safety

GIS is making emergency management faster and more accurate in responding to natural disasters, providing a comprehensive and effective system of preparedness, mitigation, response, and recovery. Case studies include GIS use in siting fire stations, routing emergency response vehicles, controlling wildfires, assisting earthquake victims, improving public disaster preparedness, and much more. ISBN 1-879102-88-9 136 pages

Open Access: GIS in e-Government

A revolution taking place on the Web is transforming the traditional relationship between government and citizens. At the forefront of this e-government revolution are agencies using GIS to serve interactive maps over their Web sites and, in the process, empower citizens. This book presents case studies of a cross-section of these forward-thinking agencies. ISBN 1-879102-87-0 124 pages

GIS in Telecommunications

Global competition is forcing telecommunications companies to stretch their boundaries as never before—requiring efficiency and innovation in every aspect of the enterprise if they are to survive, prosper, and come out on top. The ten case studies in this book detail how telecommunications competitors worldwide are turning to GIS to give them the edge they need. ISBN 1-879102-86-2 120 pages

Conservation Geography: Case Studies in GIS, Computer Mapping, and Activism

This collection of dozens of case studies tells of the ways GIS is revolutionizing the work of nonprofit organizations and conservation groups worldwide as they rush to save the earth's plants, animals, and cultural and natural resources. As these pages show clearly, the power of computers and GIS is transforming the way environmental problems and conservation issues are identified, measured, and ultimately, resolved. ISBN 1-58948-024-4 252 pages

GIS Means Business, Volume Two

For both business professionals and general readers, *GIS Means Business, Volume Two* presents more companies and organizations, including a chamber of commerce, a credit union, colleges, reinsurance and real estate firms, and more, who have used ESRI software to become more successful. See how businesses use GIS to solve problems, make smarter decisions, enhance customer service, and discover new markets and profit opportunities. ISBN 1-58948-033-3 188 pages

CONTINUED ON NEXT PAGE

Other books from **ESRI Press** *continued*

ESRI Software Workbooks

Understanding GIS: The ARC/INFO® Method
(UNIX®/Windows NT® version)
A hands-on introduction to geographic information system technology. Designed primarily for beginners, this classic text guides readers through a complete GIS project in ten easy-to-follow lessons.
ISBN 1-879102-01-3 608 pages

Understanding GIS: The ARC/INFO Method (PC version)
ISBN 1-879102-00-5 532 pages

ARC Macro Language: Developing ARC/INFO Menus and Macros with AML
ARC Macro Language (AML™) software gives you the power to tailor ARC/INFO Workstation software's geoprocessing operations to specific applications. This workbook teaches AML in the context of accomplishing practical ARC/INFO Workstation tasks, and presents both basic and advanced techniques. ISBN 1-879102-18-8 826 pages

Getting to Know ArcView GIS
A colorful, nontechnical introduction to GIS technology and ArcView software, this workbook comes with a working ArcView demonstration copy. Follow the book's scenario-based exercises or work through them using the CD and learn how to do your own ArcView project.
ISBN 1-879102-46-3 660 pages

Extending ArcView GIS
This sequel to the award-winning *Getting to Know ArcView GIS* is written for those who understand basic GIS concepts and are ready to extend the analytical power of the core ArcView software. The book consists of short conceptual overviews followed by detailed exercises framed in the context of real problems. ISBN 1-879102-05-6 540 pages

Getting to Know ArcGIS Desktop: Basics of ArcView, ArcEditor,™ and ArcInfo
Getting to Know ArcGIS Desktop is a workbook for learning ArcGIS,™ the newest GIS technology from ESRI. Readers learn to use the software that forms the building blocks of ArcGIS: ArcMap™ for displaying and querying maps; ArcCatalog™ for managing geographic data; and ArcToolbox™ for setting map projections and converting data. Richly detailed illustrations and step-by-step exercises teach basic GIS tasks. Includes a fully functioning 180-day trial version of ArcView 8 software on CD–ROM, as well as a CD of data for working through the exercises. ISBN 1-879102-89-7 552 pages

ESRI educational products cover topics related to geographic information science, GIS applications, and ESRI technology. You can choose among instructor-led courses, Web-based courses, and self-study workbooks to find education solutions that fit your learning style and pocketbook. Visit www.esri.com/education for more information.

ESRI Press publishes a growing list of GIS-related books. Ask for these books at your local bookstore or order by calling 1-800-447-9778. You can also shop online at www.esri.com/gisstore. Outside the United States, contact your local ESRI distributor.

ESRI Press • 380 New York Street • Redlands, California 92373-8100 • www.esri.com/esripress